ONLY
TRADiES
IMPROVE
RELIABILITY

GERARD WOOD

ONLY TRADiES IMPROVE RELIABILITY

EFFECTIVE TRADES CULTURE

First published in 2026 by Dean Publishing
PO Box 119
Mt. Macedon, Victoria, 3441
Australia
deanpublishing.com

DEAN PUBLISHING

Cataloguing-in-Publication Data
National Library of Australia
Title: Only Tradies Improve Reliability
ISBN: 978-1-764372-36-7
Category: Business/Trade and Industry

Cover concept originated from Amy Tejada.
Final cover design and layout by Dean Publishing.

I'd like to acknowledge the skilled hands (and minds) of the tradies. Whether their expertise is electrical, mechanical, welding, fitting, plumbing, or building, tradies keep our industries running. I'd also like to pay a special tribute to the people who taught me what quality really looks like.

CONTENTS

INTRODUCTION

A Recipe for
Reliability

"RELIABILITY IS BUILT BY TRADIES WHO TAKE PRIDE IN WHAT THEY DO."

L ong before I became a consultant helping mining companies improve the reliability of their equipment, I worked as a tradie. In those days, more than 30 years ago, tradesmen like me took pride in keeping our machines running reliably. We never wanted to come into work and learn from the night shift that one of our machines had broken down, as they would let you know in no uncertain terms that you had made a mistake and caused them dramas (or worse, interrupted their sleep!). That made you feel terrible, so you did everything you could to prevent that from happening.

It was just part of the culture.

What was different about our workplace in those days was that each of us was responsible for the same part of the machine every service day. We did the same preventative maintenance inspections and adjustments on the same equipment every fortnight. We got to know our machines extremely well. We knew which ones needed additional attention, the rate of deterioration of defects, and when it was essential to take corrective action to prevent a breakdown.

Many years later, Martin Grant, a former colleague, conducted a study of our site and four others to determine why our site experienced fewer unscheduled maintenance events and consistently had higher availability than the others. He considered many factors: the age of the equipment, reliability processes, shutdown processes, budget, and the number and experience level of the tradies. He concluded that the only difference between the sites was the culture. Ours was the only operation where the mechanics and electricians consistently focused on the same area of each machine. At other sites, the tradies worked on whatever job they were assigned, regardless of which machine was on service. This meant that if there was a breakdown, no single person would be held accountable, nor would they even realise it was an omission on their part that allowed the breakdown to occur.

Assigning mechanics to specific equipment enabled them to become experts while also building in accountability. We took ownership of our equipment. We appreciated its quirks and fretted about its shortcomings. We compared notes with tradies managing similar machines, creating both good-natured competition and a support network. No one wanted the equipment assigned to them to fail, and many of us went the extra mile to ensure it did not. We did not realise it at the time, but we had created a special culture that made us the highest-performing site in the company.

WHO IS THIS BOOK FOR?

This book is for two readers: tradies and managers. I have been in both roles and understand the challenges people in each face.

Whether you are called a tradie, artisan, technician, mechanic, service person, or craftsman, the insights in this book are designed to help you get more satisfaction from your work, gain a heightened sense of pride in the vital role you play, and manage difficult organisational cultures. More importantly, this book will show you how to embrace your role with pride and confidence. No matter how well-crafted the strategy or how detailed the work instructions are, reliability is built by the quality of work you deliver with your own two hands and curious mind.

Unfortunately, I have seen many workplaces where the culture does not value quality work, and I know this significantly detracts from many tradies' job satisfaction. One of my goals with this book is to convince tradies and their managers to collaborate better to create workplaces where quality work is expected, acknowledged, and rewarded. The most honourable trade role should be the one where people do the mundane, regular service inspections, adjustments, and cleaning tasks.

This includes all who do these tasks: the tradies, operators, and servicepeople. These are the roles that keep the machines breakdown-free, but they are often overlooked. Too often, the tradies who fix breakdowns get the most recognition.

It is also essential that leaders and managers read this book. It is the manager's responsibility to create the culture that enables tradies to do their best work and deliver reliable equipment. Managers should treat this book in two ways: as a tool to help them understand how to create an effective trade culture that delivers organisational outcomes, and as a resource they can share with the tradies they manage. Providing your workers with their own copy of this book is an excellent way to convey the respect you have for them and the expectations you have of their work. That kind of culture makes the leadership role significantly more rewarding. Moreover, that kind of respect fosters a workplace where tradies do not just identify problems; they also identify solutions, leading to greater accountability, better decision-making after hours, and ownership. Sometimes it is easy to forget about the trade culture, and this book will serve as a reminder to you and your tradies of the critical nature of their work.

Too often, I have heard maintenance and engineering leaders (including me) saying, "We need X number of fitters for that job," without considering what skills or experience the fitters need for the task at hand. Just getting any old fitter and throwing them at the task will create vastly different outcomes and vastly different equipment reliability than when you selectively choose the specific fitter who is experienced with the problem you are facing. When I was a supervisor, I allocated only the right people to critical tasks to get the best reliability outcomes.

Regardless of the approach you use, I hope readers of this book will improve their work satisfaction and foster an environment that inspires the next generation of tradies, artisans, craftspeople, and technicians to take pride in well-maintained equipment and the improved business outcomes that follow.

WHY I WROTE THIS BOOK

Seventeen years into my career, I had worked in all the line management roles in maintenance. I was a tradie first, then a supervisor, a maintenance planner, a superintendent, an engineer (after I completed my engineering degree over a decade), and then a maintenance manager. I then moved into central (corporate) maintenance improvement roles and learnt much more about reliability improvement theories. I facilitated reliability-centered maintenance (RCM) and preventative maintenance optimisation (PMO) projects, taught root cause analysis (RCA) programs across many of our company sites, and facilitated many other improvement programs.

Many worthwhile improvement projects emerged from these activities, well-supported by high-quality data and excellent processes. However, I could not understand why the reliability of the mining equipment fleets and processing plants across the company barely improved. The top five areas of downtime and chronic failures were also consistent and barely changed over the years. These problems were consistently occurring in basic components, including electrical systems, electrical sensors, hydraulic hoses, engine components, and accessories. There were some minor fleet improvements for a period, but nothing that sustainably improved reliability across the company. My curiosity got the better of me, and I had to dig deeper.

I visited the sites and reviewed what the reliability

engineers were doing. They were doing great improvement projects, just as they had been taught, tracking the improvement actions and only closing the projects after a problem had been eliminated. So why was the overall equipment performance about the same? After digging deeper, I realised it was due to the inconsistent quality or random execution of the current maintenance programs, work procedures, and checklists. By the time one chronic failure area had been fixed, another had started. By the time these had been corrected, the original chronic failures had returned. This cycle occurred over many years, so by the time the original failures had returned, there was a new reliability engineer in the role, and they did not realise it was a recurring problem (same problem, different day!).

What I learnt was that most problems were related to the trades culture. It was not the checklists, training, skill level, manpower, timing, or equipment. The reason chronic failures recur is due to a weak maintenance execution culture. In this case, tradies were not taking ownership of the equipment, and managers were not holding them accountable, or even worse, management decisions were preventing tradies and operators from taking pride in and ownership of 'their' machines. Our equipment was unreliable because the people maintaining it were not being held to a clear, consistent standard. For example, no one was double-checking critical alignment or bolting tasks. Managers had to take responsibility for failing to maintain a culture of high standards. Tradies had to take responsibility, too, for the sloppy workmanship that resulted, as they were not upholding high standards either.

Throughout my career, I have seen tens of millions of dollars invested by companies in RCM, PMO, and RCA programs that produced little or no sustainable improvement. I felt I could change that, so in 2010 – after 21 years in line maintenance roles and 5 years in central improvement teams – I founded Bluefield Asset Management Specialists. Our goal was to deliver practical services for maintenance managers that added value. How did we define practical services? After some discussion, we agreed that it meant services that made a difference at the trade level and improved equipment performance. I was very proud of the team we developed in Bluefield; the improvement projects we implemented helped sites create a quality trade culture that quickly increased equipment reliability and decreased costly breakdowns. Bluefield joined Deloitte Australia in 2021, and after a few years, this freed me to find other ways to help more businesses and teams improve.

That's the goal of this book. I hope that by sharing my experiences, I can reach many more people than I ever could in a consulting capacity. In my experience, equipment reliability problems in many industries will not improve until we improve company cultures by allowing tradies to take pride in their work and holding them accountable for meeting quality standards. I have seen that ideal deliver results, and I know it requires managers and tradies to work together. Capital-intensive industries can make sustainable improvements in equipment reliability – and by extension, their bottom-line – when we empower tradies to demand higher standards and uphold the traditions of quality workmanship that have historically characterised their field. Managers need to do their part by raising the bar and creating an environment and culture where good work is expected and rewarded.

I wrote this book so fundamental practices can be more widely understood. These practices are often taken for granted as being in place, but they are rarely implemented effectively. Without these fundamentals, there is zero path to sustainable reliability improvement.

Without creating this culture, the content of my next book, *Accelerating Reliability Improvement*, will not be as effective.

I also want to spotlight the importance of tradies, craftspeople, and artisans globally. These roles are essential for efficient companies and an effective society, but their significance is often overlooked by management. Supervisors often talk about how many tradies they need for a job, but rarely about the skills those tradies must have to do a quality job. There is a big difference between someone with the qualification and someone who is a craftsperson known for their quality work. Organisations that recognise this perform well and have reliable assets.

WHAT YOU WILL LEARN

This book is not about creating maintenance schedules or training new workers. Instead, it is aimed at helping managers get better work from their tradespeople, enlist tradies' help in preventing breakdowns, and create a culture where tradies enjoy their work more and are inspired to do their best work. Along the way, you will also learn:

- **Improving reliability improves your bottom line** by reducing turnover and training costs and minimising costly, unscheduled downtime.
- **Why tradies do not always do quality work.** It is not because they do not have the training or experience; it is because they either do not know how to fix something, the culture they work in emphasises speed or cost over quality workmanship, or they simply overlook the problem areas because they think the condition is somehow acceptable.
- **Methods for improving the workplace culture.** Tradies should be encouraged to spot developing problems and perform at a high level. This can be accomplished with productive, engaged meetings, visual management boards, and routine communications that help develop a shared understanding of what constitutes quality workmanship.
- **Tradies must take some responsibility for their workplace culture.** As a tradie, doing the bare minimum and resenting the supervisor does nothing for the company nor for your personal mindset. While going above and beyond is

something you should do for yourself, it just happens to also be good for the company. Which type of worker do you want to be?

- **TLC and TCDC** – and why these simple acronyms can help mechanical, electrical, and welding tradies do quality work.

WHAT IS A TRADIE?

I use the term 'tradies' to describe the skilled individuals who perform the hands-on work that keeps our equipment running and our businesses productive. Outside of Australia, they are often known as tradespeople, artisans, craftspeople, mecánicos, eléctricos, operators, or technicians. Regardless of the term, these are the people responsible for the practical aspects of maintenance, installation, servicing, and repair, ensuring that machines, systems, and infrastructure operate as intended.

The term 'tradie' holds a special place in Australian culture. It evokes images of hardworking individuals who take pride in their craft, are willing to tackle tough jobs, bring valuable expertise to their work, and are often known for their playful approach. This term is exclusive to Australia, but wherever I have worked – Africa, the Americas, Canada, and Asia – these roles share a common culture, and the individuals all desire a workplace where precision and care are valued. Whether you are a mechanical fitter in Western Australia, an electrical technician in South America, or a welder in Africa, your work is what determines whether the equipment thrives or fails.

A tradie's role is far more than just 'fixing things'. In fact, we will learn that their role is also to prevent equipment failures and improve reliability. Tradies implement all the work designed by engineers, supervisors, planners, and equipment manufacturers. This is why reliability cannot be achieved without a trade culture that demands high-quality standards. Tradies are the last link in the chain, and their work determines equipment reliability, regardless of what was done or intended before the task was executed.

THE SECRET TO RELIABILITY

I know the title of this book – *Only Tradies Improve Reliability* – may be controversial for some readers. This is intentional. It does not mean I do not value the other essential roles in the reliability improvement process.

I have always advocated for reliability engineers in the workplace. Reliability engineers can add significant value when the maintenance execution team cannot solve a problem. I saw the benefits of incorporating reliability engineers into the industry decades ago. Their greater analytical and data analysis skills can help teams focus better, identify the real cause of chronic failures that seem unstoppable, and design out problems when that course of action is required.

While I have seen the value reliability engineers bring to equipment performance, I think we often overlook the critical role that tradies play in ensuring our machinery and fleets run dependably. Their repair work must be flawless or at the highest level of quality, and we need safeguards that check and ensure it is. But the tradies' job does not end there. To sustain reliability, mechanics must also be skilled problem-solvers who can analyse symptoms, interpret failure conditions, and help deduce the cause of a failure. In many ways, they are the best people to play this role because it is their hands tightening the bolts, adjusting alignments, and performing quality welds. They understand the equipment better than anyone, and we need a workplace culture that recognises this and holds tradies responsible for sharing their critical insights.

Some years ago, I wrote a paper titled 'The 9 Mistakes Businesses Make with Reliability Engineers'. The intent of this paper and, in part, this book is to enable reliability engineers to be effective. Reliability engineers are not there to fix things but to proactively anticipate problems and design ways to avert them. They should not be bogged down with immediate breakdowns when they should be looking for larger, systemic problems. They need to work hand in glove with tradies, in a sense, so they can share ideas, data, and observations.

For that to happen, engineers must value the tradies' expertise and experience, and tradies must adopt a shared accountability for the trustworthiness of the equipment they work on. They are two sides of the same coin, each bringing unique perspectives and skills to the table. When they work together seamlessly, it creates a powerful synergy that drives continuous improvement. Many years ago, in a mining fleet maintenance department, we enlisted our first reliability engineer. We already had good machine reliability, but we often had short breakdowns on the dragline and shovel ground-engagement tools (the buckets and teeth that dug the dirt). These breakdowns were due to the keepers cracking and falling out, allowing the tooth to fall off the bucket or the chain anchor pin to fall out. We had normalised it in our culture and were great at executing quick repairs. The engineer, however, saw that we could get another 2 percent per annum in availability if we eliminated these breakdowns. He discussed the problems with the boilermakers (welders) who installed the keepers. In those days, they were all welded in place. The boilermaker said he knew the breakdowns were occurring because the keepers had not been welded correctly. They did a cold weld, and it created a stress point that would easily crack. He worked with the engineer to design a much better keeper installation welding process and to allocate time and equipment to ensure these quality welds happened consistently. It was an excellent outcome for everyone. The company saw improved equipment performance; the engineer was satisfied with his impact, and most of all, the tradies felt satisfied that they were doing quality work and making a significant impact.

1

The Value of Effective Trades Cultures

"A GREAT TRADES
CULTURE TURNS
ORDINARY
WORKPLACES
INTO ECONOMIC
BUSINESSES
WHERE PEOPLE
WANT TO STAY."

In my last role as a maintenance manager, we had a large fleet of trucks, including Caterpillar 789 haul trucks. Fleet availability was around 89 percent – not great, but not bad either. Our site had good planning and reliability processes, but the unscheduled downtime was costing the company money. Less material could be mined, and the frequent downtime created a bottleneck in the chain of interconnected processes at the mining site. As everyone knows, reactive maintenance that occurs during unscheduled downtime is more costly than planned maintenance. When critical equipment fails unexpectedly, it never occurs at a convenient time or in a convenient location. You lose revenue from halted production while paying for 24-hour support, expedited parts, and idle labour while operators wait for their machines to be fixed.

To improve the reliability and availability of the trucks, we revised the fleet-wide maintenance strategy. We adjusted the scheduled downtime to coincide with the rosters of the tradies who worked on the trucks. We performed oil and filter changes based on engine hours, but reduced this service process to a maximum of 4 hours by removing tasks and making the essential tasks efficient with the correct tooling. We moved all other tasks to a 24-hour scheduled service day every 24 days so the same team was rostered on and the same people could work on the same machine. Once we had established this strategy, ownership of the machines increased; the tradies' ability to track defect progress improved, and a culture of quality execution emerged. The fleet availability subsequently improved to 94 percent. This 5 percent improvement in fleet availability was equivalent to an additional truck, and the downtime removed was unscheduled, making it even more valuable to the business.

THE EFFECT OF REMOVING CHRONIC BREAKDOWNS

During my Bluefield days, a maintenance manager at one site with a large fleet of Liebherr T282 trucks wanted and expected the fleet to be available more than 90 percent of the time. When we arrived, several people said that the goal could not be achieved. They said there were too many chronic breakdowns caused by the machine's design, but our analysis indicated that many of those breakdowns were due to poor execution of their current PM (preventative maintenance) program. Oil leaks developed because new O rings in service kits were difficult to install and frequently discarded; strut pressure checks were performed incorrectly, leading to failures; grease tanks were incorrectly filled and grease systems poorly maintained, and oil cleanliness often fell outside established targets. Moreover, checks, adjustments, and inspections to prevent these problems from becoming breakdowns were not being carried out correctly.

When we presented these findings, the maintenance superintendent, supervisors, and some of the tradies were displeased, somewhat embarrassed, and slightly angry with us. However, we discussed what we found and reviewed the evidence, which was clear and incorporated many examples from their maintenance records and executed PM checklists. They had to accept the facts and worked with us to create actions and working agreements they felt were needed to address the problems we had identified. In particular, one of these actions was to discuss work execution quality at each shift-start meeting and to significantly raise the culture around work quality standards. They decided to show photos of good and bad practices at each shift-start meeting with the maintenance teams.

However, in a follow-up review a month later, I

discovered none of these actions and agreements had been adequately implemented. I raised a red flag with the superintendent and supervisors because they had told me the actions were implemented. In a meeting with everyone, and although the superintendent believed the new approach had been implemented, one of the tradies claimed he had never heard of any new actions or agreements, nor the shift-start meeting process. Neither had the guys in the workshop.

At that point, the superintendent actually took ownership and implemented the actions and agreements as we discussed. When I returned 2 months later, the superintendent was present at the shift-start meetings to coach the supervisor who ran these meetings on how to ensure the desired culture was created by discussing good and bad execution practices. It was great to see, and while the superintendent was still unhappy with me and the comments I made on the last trip to the site, he fully owned what they were doing. Within 6 months, the fleet hit 90 percent availability and stayed there or above for at least 4 years, after which we stopped tracking the data. Increasing the fleet availability from 85 percent to above 90 percent meant 17,520 additional operating hours per annum, or the equivalent of three more trucks in the fleet, directly increasing the tons of material hauled. The site manager and superintendents were so impressed with the improvements they asked us to roll out the same program for their other fleets and fixed plant assets.

One of the most memorable moments of this project came months later, when one of the supervisors told me he had hated my review, but the subsequent process that followed was his best career experience to that point. He had committed to improving execution; reliability had increased, and his team had come together to enjoy the success. And it had all resulted from people taking responsibility for the current breakdowns and creating a culture of quality work execution! Years later, a maintenance superintendent also told me that many people had come from other sites the company owned to see how they had made the improvements. They all seemed to take away the shiny visual boards and visible conditions in the workshop, but few realised that the changes were just part of the culture that had been created. Changing the shift-start boards and cleaning the workshop do not change the culture; these things emerge from creating the correct culture first.

THE MONETARY BENEFITS

A strong record of equipment reliability is not just a 'nice-to-have' for any asset-intensive company; it is a pillar of its financial success and sustainability. The demanding, often remote, nature of critical assets in any industry means reliable equipment translates directly into significant fiscal benefits:

- **Increased production:** Reliable equipment with fewer breakdowns means more operating hours and more output for the same asset base.
- **Consistent output:** Predictable equipment performance allows for more stable production schedules and targets, reducing variability and enabling the company to meet its supply commitments consistently.
- **Extended component life:** Proactive strategies and execution cultures help prevent catastrophic failures and extend the lifespan of costly components. You can also defer expensive new capital investments when your equipment lasts longer. The ROI (return on investment) on your assets improves significantly.
- **Safer workplace:** Equipment failures can often

create dangerous situations. Being reactive often leads people to make unsafe decisions, as they perceive it to be in the company's best interest. A strong reliability program lowers the risk of worker injury and fatality.

- **Proactive maintenance:** Fixing minor defects is *always* cheaper than waiting for failure.
- **Reduced stress:** A reactive environment puts stress on maintenance teams who are constantly dealing with emergencies rather than systematic work. This can lead to burnout, high turnover, and reduced job satisfaction, which are a significant cost or source of loss and waste for companies.

Everyone in asset-intensive industries or industries that have large teams of tradies recognises there is significant monetary value in getting reliable equipment and getting the work done well the first time to reduce or eliminate re-work. The experiences shared in this chapter are among the most memorable and valuable of my career, and the improvements were so successful because of the focus on the trades culture. There are many more stories from my own experience and from others who have shared their experiences with me, so I hope the takeaway is clear – an effective trades culture is an essential and valuable part of any asset-intensive business.

Apart from the significant business value from increased equipment uptime, such as improving a plant or fleet availability by 5 percent, another great outcome from the workplaces whose stories I share in this chapter was that everyone involved in these improvements benefited. Their personal career opportunities improved significantly. When plants and equipment perform at high standards, as presented here, the people involved are always in high demand from other employers. This was true for everyone involved in these sites. Not only were the people in leadership roles able to advance their careers over time, but the tradies who were part of these teams were able to get jobs anywhere they wanted, as they could discuss these experiences and outcomes, which every business desires.

Increased plant uptime is valuable to all industries with assets. The impact of breakdowns is always a cost, even in a small business. When tradies work in an effective culture, they experience job satisfaction, and turnover is significantly reduced. My experience has shown that trade culture, specifically a focus on the quality of the work tradies execute, is the critical ingredient for achieving both increased uptime and an effective culture where employees want to stay.

2

Why Tradies Do NOT Always Do Quality Work

"MOST FAILURES
AREN'T CAUSED
BY TRADIES WHO
DON'T KNOW OR
DON'T CARE.
THEY'RE CAUSED
BY TRADIES
WHO DON'T SEE
THE ISSUE."

When I was in my last line role as a maintenance manager, I walked past a very experienced fitter drilling out a broken bolt in an engine component. I stopped and looked, because something wasn't quite right. He said to me, "I should have the orifices covered, correct?"

I agreed. Drilling swarf could come off the drill bit and lodge inside these open areas, which must remain pristine, or they could cause the engine to fail once reinstalled. The guy was one of the best fitters, had a good attitude, and knew better. Yet he had cut corners and was taking a huge risk with the engine's potential failure. Why?

Over the years of working with many teams, I have concluded that there are three possible reasons tradies do not do a quality job the first time:

- They don't know.
- They don't care.
- They don't see.

Understanding each reason is crucial to developing solutions that will significantly improve the work culture and work satisfaction for everyone on the team.

DON'T KNOW

'Don't know' refers to situations where a tradie simply lacks the technical knowledge required to do the job correctly. While this can sometimes cause breakdowns, the surprising truth is that complex gaps in technical knowledge do not cause most reliability issues. Instead, they are the result of how tradies are taught in the first years of their apprenticeships.

Think about the breakdowns you have seen in your career. How often are they caused by missed alignment steps, hoses fitted incorrectly, or leaks left unaddressed? These are not advanced engineering challenges; they are the basics of good trade work, things we all learnt as apprentices. I have done breakdown Pareto analysis to identify the main areas causing breakdowns far too many times in my career. Every time, whether the analysis was for mobile plant or fixed plant, at least 50 percent of the breakdown time was caused by short-duration chronic events, which are also the easiest to correct because they are nearly always due to the basic trade skills not being executed correctly.

Yes, we can and should continuously update our tradies' technical skills. Providing technical training from equipment suppliers is essential, and there should be ongoing training plans to ensure the team always has adequate technical knowledge. I am sure some significant issues that caused major component failures were due to a lack of knowledge. However, I struggle to recall many examples of these from my career. The ones I do recall were related to the original equipment manufacturer (OEM), quality manufacture, or new equipment with failure modes unknown to us, such as not controlling the operating conditions and suffering failures due to over-loading or less tolerance to lubrication contamination. The OEMs, having all the necessary deep equipment technical knowledge, have always helped resolve these problems, and that knowledge can easily be passed on to the equipment owner. Each area should have detailed trade technical skills matrices managed by the supervisors. Sometimes the required skills are best obtained by deliberately allocating to specific tasks rather than more in-class training time. The supervisor should know each team member's technical skills and work to continually improve them.

Sometimes we see breakdowns, and we assume they result from a lack of knowledge. I was once reviewing a site and found that many breakdowns were due to conveyor braking systems. The brake thrusters were failing to lift in time or set in time, which caused a trip in the control system logic. There were several issues around setting the correct level of oil in the thruster, and ensuring the oil in the thrusters was clean and the filters were maintained correctly. These types of events can make leaders think there is a knowledge gap, and at this site, there was training being organised with the conveyor brake system suppliers. But in reality, tradies learn early in their apprenticeships that keeping oil clean, replacing filters, and filling oil compartments correctly is essential. These points were, at worst, forgotten by the site. When these types of issues are discussed daily, as proposed in chapter three, everyone is reminded of the correct quality principles, and their knowledge is elevated as a result. After the first failure, when the oil is found to be low, it should be discussed at the shift-start meeting to remind everyone of the importance of these tasks.

Even on mining sites built in remote areas where mining is new, developing local tradies to an adequate level of knowledge, supported by 'knowledge experts' for a period of time, takes only a few years. The key to success here is to have the support of knowledge experts who also uphold quality standards above the norm.

Later in this book, I will cover key maintenance principles that reinforce the right quality mindset for mechanical, electrical, and welding trades as they conduct PM activities. Still, before we blame 'don't know' as the root cause of breakdowns, we should first ask whether we are making the most of the trade skills our teams already have, and whether we are actually implementing the current PM programs as they were intended.

In reality, and I have analysed the data many times to prove this point, most tradies possess the technical knowledge required to prevent the most common failures or at least failures that represent 50 percent of the breakdown time. The challenge is not around what they know; it is in ensuring they apply their knowledge consistently. This leads us to the next factor: 'don't care'.

DON'T CARE

When you hear the phrase, "They just don't care," it is easy to jump to conclusions. Are there tradies who genuinely do not care? Perhaps, but they are rare. From what I have seen, most tradies care deeply about how their work is perceived. They want respect from their peers, supervisors, and company leaders, and they take pride in their work.

If you see a workplace where tradies appear not to care about quality, it is more likely that this attitude has been shaped by the environment they are in. When leaders fail to set clear expectations, when the focus is only on speed or cost rather than quality, or when people feel like their efforts are ignored or undervalued, that is when a 'don't care' perception can take hold. In reality, it is rarely a lack of care. Instead, it is a lack of connection to the outcome. In my last line role, if I had created a stronger culture of quality and made quality visible, maybe the tradie I mentioned would have taken the time to properly cover the orifices. I have to accept the responsibility for not creating the right culture in that workplace.

Improving this mindset is not about lecturing tradies to care more; it is about creating a culture where quality is visible, valued, recognised, and rewarded. Leaders must actively shape the environment so pride in workmanship becomes the norm. Part of doing this, however, involves also making poor quality visible. Tradies want to know that poor-quality work is addressed equally and that team members are mutually accountable to do good work so others do not have to fix the outcomes of inferior work.

Making quality visible and creating a culture of mutual accountability is both simple and difficult. Chapter three is dedicated to unpacking this, and the methods I propose are all simple to implement and have been proven many times over to work. The difficult part is having the emotional maturity to implement them without creating a negative experience for all. When done correctly, it should be a positive experience that builds a positive team culture, uplifts ownership, and clearly defines the unacceptable standards.

DON'T SEE

Of the three causes, 'don't see' is the most common and the most easily overlooked. Often, the quality issue is not that someone lacked knowledge or did not care; they simply did not see the problem.

I remember when I was a young electrician working on dragline maintenance. One day, an inspector visited the site and found holes in several electrical cabinets where some overload reset buttons had been removed. The inspector insisted the machine could not return to work until those holes were properly sealed. At the time, I thought he was being unreasonable. Why stop the machine for something that seemed so minor? But over time, I realised he had the right mindset. He could see something I had taken for granted as normal.

I had not ignored the problem out of laziness or apathy; I just did not see it as an issue because that is how the equipment looked when I first arrived. It became 'normal' to me. This is the danger of 'don't see'. If no one ever highlights the flaws, those conditions become the accepted standard.

In recent years, I visited a site and walked past an open electrical cabinet with the site supervisor. When I saw that the door was slightly open, I immediately stopped. The open door was due to a lock installed inside the cabinet to isolate a circuit that was no longer in service, which prevented the door from closing and sealing. I was there to assist them in reducing electrical downtime events, and dust ingress was one of the key issues! The supervisor immediately recognised it was not an acceptable standard and was allowing dust ingress. He said he had walked past it so many times it had become invisible to him.

Our standards are often shaped by the conditions we inherit. When we start working in an environment with loose cables, patched-up temporary repairs, or oil leaks around every corner, we begin to think those conditions are standard, even acceptable. But they are not. The first step to improving quality is to make those issues visible.

At another site, I conducted a review and found a critical hydraulic unit controlling the site bottleneck equipment that was full of leaks, spare hoses full of dirt and dust, and oil overheating. It was clearly in a terrible state. I looked at the previous year's monthly PM inspection checklists, and they all indicated very few problems. When I raised this in a meeting with the supervisors and tradies and showed the photos, there was a lot of discomfort in the room. I kept asking how it could be in this condition. There were no subsequent actions to correct the condition and no indication on the PM checklists of the actual condition. Eventually, one of the tradies broke and said in a very frustrated manner, "It has been like that for ages. We tried to get it corrected, but no one ever took any action, so we just ignore it."

Nothing frustrates tradies more than a culture that seemingly ignores their feedback on inspections or disregards the defects they have raised. This is the single best way to create a culture where tradies 'don't see' because they assume the defects raised are acceptable. Someone in this meeting suggested that we needed better PM checklists with photos of what good conditions look like (they thought the problem was 'don't know' related). "Really?" I said. "What if the office accountant, with no maintenance experience, were to look at the plant? Would they know the conditions aren't good?" They agreed, yes, it was apparent. So, telling experienced tradies this level of detail would be like telling them how to suck eggs. All that was needed was the mutual understanding of the acceptable standards within the plant.

As an example of the same issue, I was recently on a hiking trip along an Australian coastal track, and the guide was pointing out all the different flora. There was a lot, and the guide could see each species individually. Initially, I could only see 'plants'. It did not take long, with an experienced eye continually pointing them out, for us to begin to see the different plants and flowers. It reminded me of a great tool to open people's eyes and allow them to see the defects. We called it a 'defect challenge', and you can download it at gerardwood.com.au/resources.

All it does is create an environment where participants are specifically looking for minor defects, taking photos of them, and then testing whether they were identified during previous PM inspections. This exercise helps develop the ability to see defects that often go unnoticed and to raise the acceptable standards on the site.

BRINGING IT TOGETHER

I have also visited many sites in my career that were achieving good reliability results. On each of these sites, regardless of the equipment type, leaders had very clear knowledge of the equipment's condition. These real conditions are reported by the tradies, as management cannot see them all. On good sites, the leadership can talk about the equipment defects that are of concern to them, and they know off the top of their head they're to address the issue over the short to medium term.

Most reliability issues are not caused by tradies lacking technical skill or by an inherent lack of care. They are caused by tradies not applying what they already know because they simply 'don't see' the issues. In my experience, the most powerful improvement comes from improving visibility, helping tradies and leaders see what quality looks like, and establishing a culture where everyone understands the acceptable standards. The cultural routines to achieve this are discussed later in the book. Creating mutual accountability for plant conditions and work standards within the team also increases job satisfaction for everyone, just as it does in successful sporting teams!

The great news is that this change does not require a massive investment or new technology. By helping tradies make quality visible and reinforcing their pride in their workmanship, we can create a powerful shift to more reliable equipment, significantly improved business outcomes, better job satisfaction, and a stronger maintenance culture.

If I were to return to a maintenance line management role now, I would immediately implement the processes and systems described in the next chapter, and I know I would see significant improvements in plant reliability and team culture. I just wish I had known this when I saw the guy drilling out the bolt all those years ago!

3

Creating the Right Culture – Management Responsibility

"REAL LEADERS
CREATE THE
CULTURE
THAT MAKES
RELIABILITY
POSSIBLE."

Everyone knows that what gets measured gets done. That has been the fundamental principle of management and systems for a long time. Unfortunately, it is not easy to measure the quality of daily maintenance work. The tradies are best placed to see it, and they will know which of their fellow tradies go the extra mile to do good quality work.

When I was in my first maintenance manager role, we allowed our tradies to hand-pick the contractors they wanted for shutdown and overhaul projects. We would request only specific people from the contractors we used for these jobs, not just anyone with the right qualifications.

Even then, it was still possible that the people doing these tasks could misfit a seal, over- or under-tension a bolt, not follow weld procedures, under-tension an electrical connection, or complete a PM checklist without really looking at the parts to be inspected. And it was also possible that no one would detect their mistake, until the machine broke down, of course!

Every time there is a breakdown, there is an opportunity to ask yourself:

- *Was this caused by our maintenance standards?*
- *How can we make this shortcoming and resulting breakdown visible to everyone so it's less likely to happen again?*

I encounter these issues repeatedly when visiting sites. Here are some memorable ones:

- A hydraulic filter started leaking in a large hydraulic hoist system. We found that the seal at the top of the large filter had failed. When I asked the tradies about it, they said there was a room full of those seals. They come as part of the service kit, but because it is a difficult job, they never get changed, and the leftover seals get thrown into the room.
- There were intermittent electrical faults on a conveyor. When I examined the junction boxes along the conveyor, I found them full of dust. The inspection and cleaning were part of the PM program, but clearly no one had ever done them correctly.
- A fire started on a truck engine after a hydraulic hose failed and sprayed oil onto the engine above

the hose. The hose was rubbing on a beam and should have been identified during the multiple service inspections.

- An access system hydraulic hose failed under a clamp. It caused the ladder on the truck to drop and the truck to stop. It turned out the hose was slightly oversized but had been fitted because it was the only one available at the time.

There are countless examples of breakdowns that could have been avoided with proper maintenance standards. I am sure anyone reading this can think of many from their experience. But what is the solution to this problem?

MAKING QUALITY VISIBLE

The solution to 'don't see' is, of course, visibility. Visibility also helps improve 'don't know' and may even improve 'don't care'. Leaders need to create routines that highlight quality problems and celebrate good quality work. Making quality visible resets expectations, teaches people who did not know a specific quality procedure, and sparks discussions that lead to greater care. Tradies who may have previously overlooked defects will begin to see them. Once they see the issues, their natural pride in their work will push them to improve. Quality eventually becomes part of the culture. This journey is not new; many industries have implemented similar processes to embed a safety culture in their organisations.

Leaders must own, lead, and demonstrate these routines, just as the maintenance superintendent did at the site I mentioned previously. Over time, however, ownership needs to transition to the teams, with the routines embedded at the trades level.

The following sections describe some simple actions we have implemented that have worked many times over. Whatever works for the business and team is the best option, and sustainable improvement comes from ownership of the process.

PHOTOS AT SHIFT-START MEETINGS

This is simple to do, but it is not easy. All that needs to be done is to bring photos of poor-quality and good-quality work to the meeting and discuss them. It is never easy to publicly discuss poor-quality work issues, and this is the biggest resistance you will encounter. The way to move past this is to discuss negative events in a way that is positive and uplifting for the team. When the supervisor or another tradie presents an example of poor-quality work they encountered, a team discussion can focus on the fact that we are better than that, and all we need to do is commit to doing things correctly.

Just like training in a sports team, we talk about where we did not execute the game as required. In the workplace, you must talk about why the work was not done correctly and what we as a team must do to improve and prevent similar problems in the future. Successful teams are willing to learn and work together to get even better than they already are. When the discussion is held this way, it actually boosts team morale. I have seen tradies in the shift-start meetings, who are usually in the back and not engaging, move forward and become very interested when these discussions are occurring. They actually see the issues, but there is no mechanism in place for them to express themselves. This is their chance, and most are eager to participate. Similarly, we should share photos of high-quality work so people can see them and repeat the same good practices. Sharing good practices equally enhances the positive nature of the meeting and reinforces the good practices that are also part of the culture.

Both situations also create mutual accountability for quality standards and quickly communicate the site's acceptable standards.

Some examples of what has been shared at other sites are:

- Photos of a task where all cleanliness controls have been implemented, ensuring that the repair does not create any contamination in the lubrication systems.
- Photos of breakdowns where the component or part failed and should have been detected during the PM program. Failed hydraulic hoses, oil leaks, and poor-quality welds are always opportunities to share.
- Photos of PM checklists that say all conditions are fine, with a subsequent photo of the actual conditions, showing leaks, loose clamps, and uncleanliness.
- Photos of critical bolts that have been torqued correctly, and the bolts marked to show any movement.

FAILED PARTS BIN

An alternative to creating a visual board with photos of good and bad quality is to have a failed parts bin near the shift-start area. This method is my personal favourite, as the tradies can review the failed part, and discussions can be held with the team to show them how it failed and why it should have been detected during the inspection program.

It is as simple as asking the tradies to put failed parts from breakdowns into the bin, with a tag indicating from where and when they were removed. At one site where we did this, a hydraulic hose had failed at the fitting. The leak was easy to see, as the hose end was wet with oil and dust that had accumulated on the oil. I reviewed the inspection sheets from the past 6 months, and there was no mention of the leak or weep. I asked the superintendent whether these hoses had failed suddenly, and he said, "No, they weep for months before failing." He was frustrated because he realised their own inspections were not being conducted correctly, and his team was not identifying defects in time to have them repaired in a scheduled manner. Instead, they were requiring costlier, more time-consuming unscheduled repairs. He had started to see the problems caused by improper inspections that he had previously assumed were being done correctly.

His plant reliability increased significantly once this team implemented the broken parts bin and improved their relationship with the planning team. One of the general managers subsequently told me he did not know what we did at that site, but he was overwhelmed by the positive change in the team culture and the equipment reliability. The site teams made changes on their own; they just needed help seeing the problems.

At another site where we implemented the same failed parts bin, there was a fuel line that had cracked under a securing clip. It had been previously repaired, and the temporary repair had caused the breakdown. When I discussed it with the mechanic who had replaced the line, he said there were no spares, so they had to take one from another truck that was in for a major repair. He noted that this line also had a previous repair in the same area, but he had to use it for the breakdown anyway.

The discussions at the shift-start meetings were informative for everyone involved. Not only had they identified an area with a clear wear-out failure mode, but they also learnt that when a temporary repair is completed, a subsequent work order must be raised to correct it properly, or it will only lead to a breakdown in the future. Allowing temporary repairs to be completed on plant and equipment is another way tradies become desensitised and do not see. All temporary repairs must have work orders raised for a positive fix to be completed. Raising them at the shift-start meetings is the key to creating a culture where everyone sees.

SIDEBAR: VISUAL BOARDS

I am sure everyone in capital-intensive industries has seen 'living dead' visual communication boards: shift-start boards or weekly meeting boards that are not updated, or where only one part is used effectively. Everyone must own these boards for them to remain alive and value-adding. I have seen sites where one person had the passion and drive behind the board, and after they left, it stopped being used. At other sites, the board was set up by a specialist consultant, and after they left, no one had the passion to continue with all the elements on the board. No wonder so many tradies check out of the shift-start process or are only there in body.

Use the shift start guideline, which can be downloaded

from gerardwood.com.au/resources, to define what the shift-start board will contain for your site.

Get some tradies and key people involved to create shared ownership of the board and process. Make sure everyone understands the significance of each element on the board and that each must be managed on an ongoing basis. Anything that is a one-off or short-term action can be accommodated in the improvement projects; they do not require a specific zone on the board. Things that need to be managed and must always be on everyone's minds need to be on the board.

As discussed previously, the hard part will be having discussions about the identified problems. First, discuss the positive areas. Starting with success stories makes discussions about failures less discouraging. The key is to acknowledge that some discussions may be difficult but are crucial to everyone's success. Being open and honest is the only way to work through any issues and gain team alignment.

In my business, we used to publish monthly utilisation figures for each employee. We recorded how many hours each person, including myself, booked for paying clients and how many were on tasks that could not be charged to clients. Some team members admitted that when their utilisation was low, it made them feel uncomfortable and like they let the team down. I said I understood, but the business is built on utilisation of our team, and publishing the numbers was never intended to create discomfort, but to create action so we could work together and ensure everyone could achieve the utilisation targets. This discussion turned a negative situation into a positive one, and people could understand that it was essential for the business.

Similarly, if low-quality work is causing breakdowns, we want to discuss it as a team so everyone learns and works together to eliminate it. Initially, however, people will feel uncomfortable if they did the work that was displayed as not meeting the standards. There will need to be a discussion about the purpose of raising it in the meeting – not to make people feel uncomfortable, but to help everyone continually improve their understanding of what is causing the breakdowns. Asset-intensive businesses need reliable assets to succeed, and eventually it also enables everyone to feel good about where they work.

ACTION ALL CONCERNS RAISED AND FEEDBACK ON PM CHECKLISTS

I once looked at a hydraulic oil-leak breakdown on a dozer in a very difficult location. The machine was down for some time while the hose was repaired.

When I looked at the previous service inspection sheets, it was noted that, three services before, some oil was coming from that area. The subsequent service inspection ticked it as all okay. The most recent said there was a lot of oil, and then the breakdown occurred about a week later. These types of breakdowns are common and create the wrong culture within the trades teams. Potentially, the second last inspection may not have been done because there was a culture of not acting on the defects detected on the service sheets.

It is the leadership's responsibility to ensure that all feedback written on PM checklists is actioned, or a discussion is held with the tradie to talk about why the actions are not required. For example, sometimes a tradie will note a defect on a service inspection, but the planning team already knows there is a work order to replace the entire component soon. This feedback should be given to the tradie so they are aware and know that their defect reporting was reviewed. Lack of action on what is written on PM checklists gives the tradies the sense that the documents are not even read. This creates a culture where no one reports defects. Digital PM checklists and inspection tools may overcome this problem, but only if the digital system is implemented with this express outcome in mind. Many of the systems I have seen implemented do not use the technology to automate the generation of subsequent work orders.

Often, tradies want to keep machines down to fix problems correctly. However, management is pressured to get the equipment back on schedule. It is essential that leadership communicates well regarding in what circumstances it is acceptable to keep machines down and extend scheduled downtime. This is usually only when not repairing the defect will cause a breakdown before the next scheduled service event.

At one site I was reviewing, the supervisor came into the office flustered. He discovered that the brake pads on a truck unexpectedly had to be replaced, as they were under the safety specification. He was rattled because it meant he had to find additional labour, the scheduled service had to be extended, and he had to get the part. In this instance, the defect should be treated like a breakdown anyway. Why was it missed, or why did it catch everyone by surprise? I looked at the previous service sheet and found that the brake pads were 0.01 mm above the minimum acceptable level (21 mm) at the last service. Fine to put back to work, but it was always going to be under spec on the next service, so a subsequent work order should have been raised then with clear priority that it had to be replaced on the next service.

Conversely, and as an extreme example, a team maintaining dozers on a site I managed initiated a repair of a dozer's worn tracks. This was not a planned task; the team just decided it needed to be done immediately. There was no risk that the tracks would fail before the next scheduled service; dozer tracks wear so slowly that there would be no noticeable difference between scheduled services, so overhauling them in an unplanned way created huge inefficiencies. The team needed to get the parts and labour mobilised, extending the dozer's downtime from a single full shift to 4 to 5 days. The correct course of action was to create a work order to replace the tracks and ensure the planning team was aware so the repair could be scheduled for the next scheduled downtime event.

Actioning feedback and treating the defects written on service and inspection sheets with the highest level of importance is critical to avoid developing a 'don't see' culture. If they sense their feedback is ignored or not even reviewed, tradies will only report things twice before checking out. Photos or examples of checklists are also great to take to the quality discussion during the shift-start meetings.

Often, we see that the tradies are responsible to open subsequent work orders, but when we review the site and find these problems, we learn there are many tradies who do not have access to the system, or no access to or time on a computer to raise the subsequent work. These become excuses, and many defects identified do not get actioned. It is the responsibility of management to overcome these issues as quickly as possible, and it should not be seen as too hard. With the number of systems we can access on phones and tablets, you would expect this to not be a problem, but for some reason, it persists.

SUMMARY OF QUALITY DISCUSSIONS

I have been to many shift-start meetings that begin with a discussion on safety and then go into a specific discussion about the day's work. Many of these meetings have very low engagement. When we implement a discussion on work quality and start showing photos or examples of good and bad quality work completed the previous day, the level of engagement immediately increases. The tradies even move closer to the supervisor and show genuine interest. This initial engagement needs to be followed up by actually engaging these tradies in the discussion and getting them talking. However, just the act of talking about their work, their trade, is enough to increase engagement at these meetings.

Sometimes, just displaying photos of the equipment condition or workplace conditions can create a mutual understanding of standards, even without supporting words. In my last line role, one of the planners went out into the workshop and parts storage areas and took about 30 photos of what he saw. He shared the photos with everyone, and without saying anything, we all knew we needed to create better housekeeping routines. We also needed an initial clean-up and organisation before implementing daily workshop inspections to ensure it did not degenerate back into this condition again. Showing us the photos and having us discuss them was all it took to get the necessary action.

There are many ways to make quality visible, and I wrote about these in another book, *Simplifying Mining Maintenance.* They are nothing new when it comes to a visual workplace and using visual boards. The process has been around in Lean and similar methodologies to improve safety and efficiency for many years, and it is still very effective in driving improvement and creating the right culture within teams.

Here are some examples of the visual tools we have used to make quality visible. It is essential that the tools and discussion are led by the leadership team initially, but ownership must then transition to the tradies. The processes are not meant to be confrontational or create tension, but instead get everyone on the same page in terms of quality work standards. Just like what we would do as a team in a post-mortem of a sporting match.

QUALITY PHOTO BOARD

The quality photo board on the next page shows an example used at one site. They simply put the photo with a title and a small description of what the issue or good practice was so everyone could understand the point. Importantly, though, it is the discussion with the teams about each photo that creates the engagement. If you want to start simply, just using a photo and talking about it at the shift-start meeting is just as effective.

QUALITY

Quality Share - Lack of Information in Work Orders

Failure:
- To capture relevant repair or troubleshooting information in work orders. Examples are EXD0215 shutdown and EXD0209 grease pump

Downtime:
- Will vary on tasks if we have to start all over again troubleshooting

Quality Issue:
- Lack of information put into notification or work order long text
- Depending on a specific group's handover (paper-based or word-of-mouth to communicate), this is a waste of time seeking out information that is not in SAP

Quality Share 28/05/2018

Relevant Procedure/Work Practice:
- As per commitments (quality data capture in SAP)

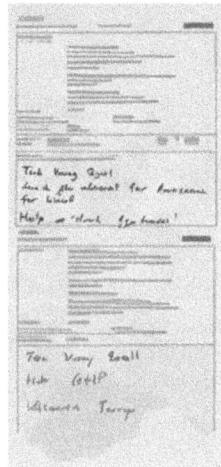

Quality Share - EXD0250 Not Setting Up for Success (Generator)

Failure:
- To connect the generator to the EXD0250 on pre-service wash

Downtime:
- Approximately 2 hours

Quality Issue:
- Generator not connected to machine for the wash period
- Batteries flattened from work lights and machine unable to start post wash

Quality Share 31/05/2018

Relevant Procedure/Work Practice:
- Service set-up requirements
- Generators available but not connected

Quality Share - 231 Grease Faults

Failure:
- Grease fault during startup after service day on 231 excavator

Downtime:
- 3 hours

Quality Issue:
- DIN plug mounted in wrong way allowing water to pool at the gland and fill the plug
- No seal at the DIN plug face allows water ingress at the solenoid coil corroding the electrical connecting pins

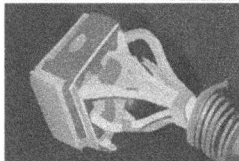

Quality Share 8/05/2018

Relevant Procedure/Work Practice:
- Inspection of devices that are rated for ingress protection must ensure that issues voiding IP rating are rectified prior to returning to work

Quality Share - EXD0217 Dog Bone Grease Lines Not Secured

Failure:
- Multiple grease lines torn off during operation

Downtime:
- 3.5 hours

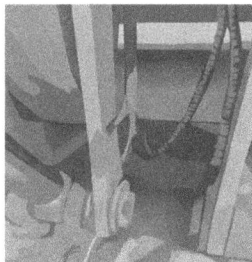

Quality Share 21/06/2018

Quality Issue:
- P clamps not fitted and lines not secured to tipping links

Relevant Procedure/Work Practice:
- Fit grease lines correctly and securely as designed

Quality Share - EXD0218 Alternator Belt Broken Shortly After Install

Failure:
- Alternator belt fit to machine 5/06/18 on service
- Belt failed 12/06/18 and new belt fit then immediately failed

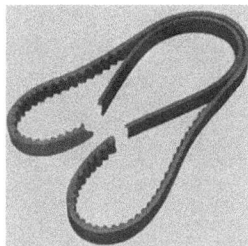

Quality Share 14/06/2018

Downtime:
- 3 hours across 3 events

Quality Issue:
- Alternator belt fitted without identifying cause
- Alternator found to have failed bearing causing loading of belt
- 3 downtime events to have positive repair

Relevant Procedure/Work Practice:
- Identifying possible root cause of alternator belt failure
- Belts changed every 4 weeks due to 6-week life expectancy so ask why belt breaks
- Inspect alternator and belt tensioner condition prior to installing belt

Quality Share - EXD0211 Fan Hoses Rubbed on Guard

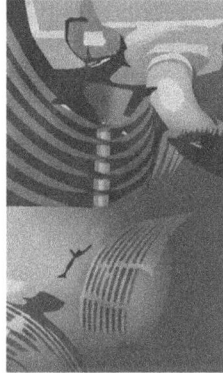

Quality Share 14/06/2018

Failure:
- PP1 fan hose rubbed on hose ferrule to point of near failure

Downtime:
- 3 hours

Quality Issue:
- Fan hoses fitted 14/03/18 including fan motor
- Fan guard bolts have fallen out allowing guard to vibrate against ferrule on HP hose
- Significant wear on ferrule shortened life and integrity of hose
- Very high risk of fire due to hose location if failure occurs

Relevant Procedure/Work Practice:
- Quality installation of all components including correct torque or securing of fan guard bolts
- Detail on inspection intervals
- Positive pick up from breakdown fitter conducting walk around inspection while on machine

QUALITY CROSS

The quality cross example on this page was used to track team quality. At each daily shift-start meeting, they would colour each box green, yellow, or red, corresponding to whether they experienced any failures due to their own work quality or their work management discipline. I prefer the photos because they tell a story and there are specific learnings associated with each photo, but whatever system works is best to use.

MAINTENANCE EXECUTION QUALITY - DAILY PERFORMANCE

TEAM

Mechanical Maintenance

MONTHLY TOP 5

DAILY PERFORMANCE

		1	2	3		
		4	5	6		
7	8	9	10	11	12	13
14	15	16	17	18	19	20
21	22	23	24	25	26	27
		28	29	30		
			31			

GREEN	YELLOW	RED
No failures due to maintenance execution or work management discipline & improvement implemented	No failures due to maintenance execution or lack of work management discipline	Failures due to maintenance execution quality or lack of work management discipline

---

BROKEN PARTS BIN

The photo on this page is of the sign that was on the front of the broken parts bin at one site. The bin was the size of a pallet, so relatively large parts could be placed in it. The sign also has instructions for use. I love this method the most, as it also encourages the tradies to touch and feel the parts. You could also use a combination of each method or invent something else that works for your team.

FAILED PARTS BIN

- Place any failed parts or components in this bin for inspection and warranty claims
- Ensure the items have an information tag attached with the following:
  - Date Removed
  - Unit #
  - Meter Reading
  - Estimated Hours Life
  - Reason For Change

This second photo is of a brake chamber that corroded out and failed in service. It had clearly been deteriorating for some time, yet the service sheets all said it was okay.

IMPLEMENTATION OF THESE METHODS

Good communication is key. As I said, all the methods mentioned have worked to build strong reliability and team culture in the past. Implementing them can be the difficult part, as good tradies who have been promoted to supervisor or superintendent roles may not be the best communicators.

The proven process to implement the methods mentioned is as follows:

- **Ownership of the solution**: First, start by identifying a problem and use several examples to discuss it with the teams. Get them to accept that change is necessary, and explain that they can suggest methods to overcome the problems. Share with them some suggested methods, such as those I have mentioned, but allow them to make the decision as to what solutions they implement. Never force them to use a method they do not accept and are willing to own.

- **Implement with support**: Once the teams agree on the method or methods to be implemented, write down who is responsible for implementing, usually the supervisors, but make sure there is a senior person who knows the required outcome to support them. For the first month at least, have the senior person attend all of the meetings and coach the supervisor as they lead the discussions.

- **Make negative situations positive**: When there is a problem, it must be discussed openly with the teams without assigning blame. No one wants to feel continually chastised for errors. When mistakes occur, they must be discussed as an opportunity to improve. It must be clear that the standards leading to the breakdown are unacceptable.

DIGITAL WORK PACKS

As mentioned, technology can help with visibility. Many organisations are implementing or using digital work packs, and now many tradies use a tablet to complete their inspections. These tools have the potential to make quality visible by automatically connecting breakdowns after the service with the defects found during the service or the lack of defects found. Zero-based maintenance (ZBM) digital tools have the appropriate principles embedded into their design. In a ZBM tool, the inspection questions are always designed to gather input (data) from the tradie about the condition, not just whether the task was completed. If the condition is outside of the set limits, a defect is automatically triggered to raise a subsequent work order, and the tradie enters the required information. Management still has the option not to approve the work order, but the workflow is transparent. If there is a breakdown after the PM, it is very simple to look in the ZBM tool history to see whether the defect was identified and whether work was approved. People who have implemented this tool say it drives greater accountability and helps change the culture.

Unfortunately, many other versions of these digital checklists are just mimicking the paper version and not extracting the full value of the technology. They only provide a list of checks and do not require any subsequent follow-up, or at least that is how many organisations choose to implement them. And do not get me started on the ERP (enterprise resource planning) systems in use. They have barely changed since I was using them in the 1990s! Some still require work order type codes, failure type codes, and codes for the area of the plant. How archaic. Have they not heard of an FMEA (failure mode and effects analysis) that should be linked to the system? I will discuss this further in my book on the future of maintenance. While digital tools offer an opportunity, they have yet to be broadly implemented with a focus on improving inspection quality and automating review when there is a failure post PM.

4

The Tradies' Responsibility

"WHEN TRADIES
TAKE PRIDE
IN EVERY JOB,
EVEN WHEN NO
ONE'S WATCHING,
THEY FEEL
BETTER ABOUT
THEMSELVES,
THEIR CAREER,
AND COMING
TO WORK."

I once attended a scheduled service day for a large excavator, and the work started 3 hours late because the night shift had allowed the machine's batteries to run flat. The service delay left 15 tradies, cleaners, and contractors waiting till the machine was jump-started and relocated, and operating inspections were completed. While I was there, several tradies complained about the situation. They said it happened often because the people cleaning the machine would not connect the generator during night-time washing.

At the shift-start meeting the next day, there was a segment to raise any concerns that needed action or improvement. No one mentioned the previous day's event. Surprised, I asked why. With such an emotive problem the day before, why not discuss it the next day and get a solution? This generated some discussion within the team, and the solution was found within minutes. This reinforced my belief that if tradies do not turn up and participate actively, meetings will not achieve their intended outcomes. Meetings are only effective when the tradies are engaged, bring information to be discussed as a team, and help with solutions, not just raise problems.

Here is the point: tradies must take some responsibility

for their workplace culture and continual improvement. Tradies who do the bare minimum are often the ones who resent the bosses and think improvement is the responsibility of others. I believe we spend too much time at work to feel miserable about it each day. When I worked as a tradie, instead of feeling that the people running the place were incompetent, I took an active role in improving things. The tradies who point out problems but also bring solutions are usually allowed to actively be part of implementing those solutions, and it makes work much more interesting and rewarding.

FOLLOW UP ON TEMPORARY REPAIRS

On one site, a chute wear plate broke off, fell, and cut the conveyor belt a long distance before the belt rip detection tripped the system. These types of conveyor belt failures are always significant in terms of downtime, spillage, and cost.

During an investigation of the incident, the reliability team found that, several months prior, during a routine inspection of the wear plates, the tradies found loose plates and had to fit some temporary bolts to hold the wear plate in place, as the correct spares were not in stock. Sometimes, as tradies, we must do temporary repairs to keep the equipment running. The issue on this occasion was, while it was recorded on the service sheet that temporary bolts had been installed, there was no subsequent work order to create a permanent fix. In some businesses, responsibility for raising subsequent work orders lies with the supervisor or planner, and the tradie can adopt a 'not my job' mentality. At this site, it was the tradies' responsibility to raise subsequent work orders, but they failed to do so, and the temporary bolts failed well before the next routine inspection. It is essential that when temporary repairs are made, there is a subsequent action to fix them so they last the required time. PM programs are built under the assumption that the equipment is as new, not full of temporary repairs.

Only the tradie knows when a temporary repair has been executed. Therefore, it is their responsibility to ensure the correct repair is done at a later date in a scheduled service period, even if they are not responsible for raising the subsequent work order.

"Fix it forever, don't be forever fixing."

GIVE GENUINE FEEDBACK ALWAYS

I was once on a site that had a problem with the suspension struts on a truck fleet having lots of short-life failures. I looked at the PM checklists on these trucks and found there was a detailed method to check the strut pressures and height, and a matrix to ensure the combination of these two was within the acceptable range. The captured results did not make sense. I went back to the tradie who had done the inspection, and he said he did not actually do it correctly because he thought it was BS, so he just placed a random dot on the matrix. He was adamant the failures were the manufacturer's fault and checks would not help. When I discussed this with the engineer who designed the inspection process (based on the manufacturer's recommendations), he said he could not prove to the manufacturer that it was their problem because he had no reliable data from inspections before the failures to show that it was maintained correctly. This highlighted to me how the tradies had mentally checked out, and there was a huge communication issue that prevented the site from progressing with these types of improvements.

Tradies must stay connected and interested and keep talking to the leaders and support staff to all align on how to best solve problems. In the case mentioned, a more open discussion about the situation to get alignment would have meant the site could have overcome the strut problem, or at least have had good data to prove to the manufacturer there were good maintenance practices and the struts were still failing.

DO NOT JUDGE, AND NEVER MENTALLY CHECK OUT

In some situations, the tradies will decide they cannot effect any change, and they mentally check out. This does not improve their enjoyment of their roles, and it widens the communication gap between management and the tradies. It is easy to judge the job your supervisor is doing, but until you have walked in their shoes, you should hold judgement.

Rather than checking out as a tradie, you can still take pride in the work you do personally. If you feel it is a waste of time and start lowering your standards, it only affects your own satisfaction. It is better to work to standards you are personally proud of, even if they are not recognised within the business. You will get some personal satisfaction, and in fact, other tradies will notice this, and you will earn their respect for your standards. You may even motivate some of them to raise their standards too!

On one site, there was a serious incident where an employee received an electric shock from a switchboard on a lighting plant. A cover plate had fallen off or was left off the switchboard, exposing the terminals inside. On a dark night when the lights were turned off, the employee was feeling around the switchboard, and his hand went inside and touched the live terminals. During the investigation, they found numerous PM checklists of the switchboard that were all ticked as good, with no defects identified. The site had developed a bad culture in which it was common for tradies to complete the PM checklists from the lunchroom without even inspecting the equipment. The switchboard had many serious defects and should not have been in service. The learning from this situation, apart from how to avoid serious legal consequences, was that the work we do as tradies can have a significant impact on the lives of our colleagues. Significant incidents like this do not happen often, but many similar situations with less serious consequences do happen regularly. These cases have led to equipment fires, equipment breakdowns, and failures of high-pressure hydraulic hoses, all potentially high-risk situations.

I do not believe any tradie would like to think their work had caused harm or increased the risk to others. The reality is, we can only keep the risks low if we always do the work to the best of our ability.

Especially when completing PM checklists, it is essential that they are done well, as they are the first line in preventing breakdowns and avoiding unsafe conditions. If you raise concerns and they do not get addressed, checking out and never raising issues again does not help improve the situation nor your personal motivation. Always do your best regardless of what others do, and you will at least feel better in yourself.

When I have worked in roles where the culture was frustrating (and we all get a chance to experience that), I used to work harder and learn more each day so I was better prepared for my next role! At least that maintained my personal motivation and happiness, even if I felt like I could not effect change where I was. As I matured, I also learnt that having conversations with other people I knew and trusted, who had been through similar situations, helped me make better decisions on how to advance.

I admit, when a site has a strong culture, it is very difficult for an individual to work in a different way. If there is a culture of going through the motions, ticking the boxes, and not really doing things correctly, then going outside of this norm is extremely uncommon. For that reason, it is essential that there is a culture designed to make this type of work quality visible. As a tradie, you can also use the practices I discussed in the previous chapter to try to effect change or make a positive difference.

When I was a tradie, I wanted to get all of the known defects on my machine corrected. The machines were a long distance from the workshop and stores, making it difficult if materials were not available to correct the defects. I often wondered why the supervisors or leaders did not do a better job, and I unintentionally judged them. I am sure this is why a lot of tradies eventually stop trying. They believe that their leadership should be doing a better job, and they get demotivated. However, once I was promoted to the supervisor role, I realised the job was not what I expected. There are always other demands on the supervisor's time that take them away from the front line and make them seem less effective. I experienced this at other levels as well throughout my career, and I realised that until you have walked in the shoes of the other role, you should not judge them nor stop contributing at your best level. In fact, a better course of action is to ask them if they see the problem you perceive and if there is anything you can do to overcome it. **Now, this course of action takes real courage, but it also delivers the greatest sense of satisfaction knowing you have given it your best effort.**

PRIDE CAN BRING PERSONAL BENEFITS

When tradies take pride in their work and do not check out, I have seen their careers advance. Some tradies like their work and do not want to be promoted, and that is fine; the world needs good, experienced tradies to stay in the trade, too! On one site where I worked on the leadership team, there was a young tradie who was very keen and always did quality work. He did not want to be promoted, as he loved being on the tools. What he did want, however, was to do interesting and challenging work. While he was on general maintenance duties, because of his level of interest and focus on quality, he was offered the opportunity to be the lead on several equipment overhauls, including trucks and loaders undergoing major component replacements and other larger defect repairs. He loved the opportunity to take a significant role in these overhauls, as it provided him with a sense of job satisfaction, especially when the equipment returned to work at an improved level of reliability. He felt a sense of personal satisfaction around how his efforts had created an improved machine. He loved the variety of work, installing new components, checking alignment, torquing bolts correctly, checking weld quality, all the elements of a true craftsperson.

In another electrical team I was involved with, there was a large installation project to fit out the electrics in a small factory. The electrical tradies involved changed a few times due to their personal circumstances. After three changes, the new tradie arrived. The factory owner wanted to gain some level of comfort with the progress and quality of the job. The new tradie reassured him he would deliver the required level of quality, but he needed time and space to get his head around the job's status and be comfortable with the work that had been done previously. While the factory owner wanted the job completed quickly, he valued the focus on quality and honesty so much he wanted only this electrician to lead the rest of the project.

When tradies demonstrate a commitment to doing a

good job, their job security always improves. Companies and individuals who work with tradies want someone they can rely on and trust to do good, quality work. This electrician was not only in high demand, but his company also paid him a premium for his time.

A mechanical tradie on yet another site was passionate about the efficiency of the work and was always raising ideas to improve work procedures to make them easier to complete and more efficient. He also had respect from the other tradies due to his passion. The company embarked on an improvement project to streamline the services on its fleet. The project's goal was to reduce the scheduled downtime for the service from 12 to 6 hours. The obvious choice for the project was this mechanic. He was able to work on this project for 1 year, creating visual tool boards, kitting the service materials, designing the task flow into four repeatable streams, and designing new tooling to make the tasks and equipment access simple. Of course, the project was a success, but the key for this person was the satisfaction in completing such a significant improvement project and working across all of the shifts to ensure the project was adopted across the entire workshop team.

5

Proactive
Maintenance

"MAINTAINING EQUIPMENT PROACTIVELY IS ALWAYS THE LEAST EXPENSIVE AND THE MOST RELIABLE METHOD. THE CHEAPEST REPAIR YOU'LL EVER DO IS THE ONE YOU PREVENT."

Some years ago, I was on a site reviewing closed work orders. I noticed a work order that had been raised and closed for adjusting belts that ran a large fan. However, the comments on the closed work order said there was no access to the fan to adjust the belts. The comments went on to say it was okay because the belts were not going to fail anytime soon! This was a clear indication of the lack of a proactive maintenance culture. Adjusting the belts would not only extend their life but also extend the life of the pulleys they drove and potentially prevent unscheduled downtime.

The model on the next page helps explain what proactive maintenance is and why it not only improves equipment reliability but also reduces maintenance costs. Some people think leaving defects until they are just about to cause a breakdown is saving money, but they do not understand physical assets. In the long run, correcting equipment condition when there are small defects costs far less than waiting until these conditions become big problems or replacing components that wear out prematurely.

The model uses a P-F curve to show the life of an asset or component. You may be familiar with the P-F curve, but if you are not, it is simply a diagram used in

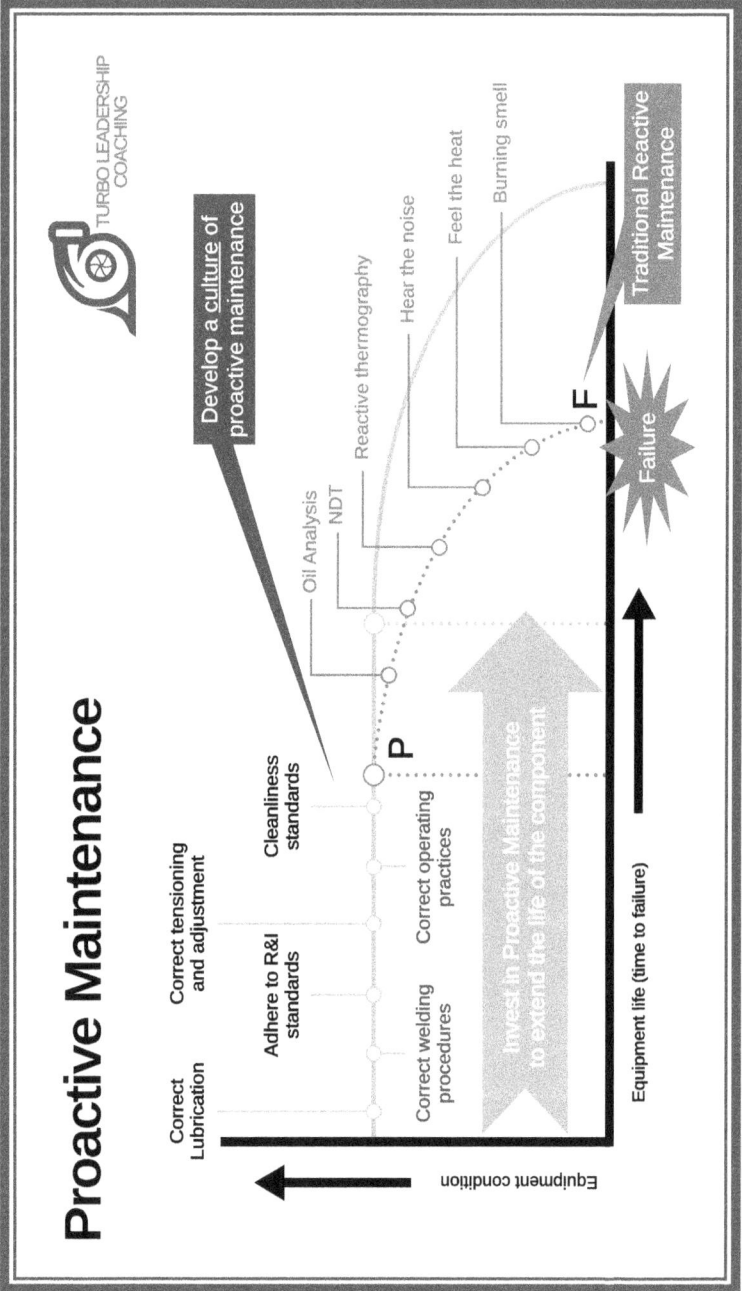

Proactive Maintenance

TURBO LEADERSHIP COACHING

Develop a culture of proactive maintenance

Correct Lubrication

Correct tensioning and adjustment

Cleanliness standards

Adhere to R&I standards

Correct welding procedures

Correct operating practices

Invest in Proactive Maintenance to extend the life of the component

Reactive thermography

Oil Analysis

NDT

Hear the noise

Feel the heat

Burning smell

P

F

Failure

Traditional Reactive Maintenance

Equipment condition

Equipment life (time to failure)

reliability theory to show where we can detect the onset of the failure mode, the P point. The earlier we detect the P point, the sooner we can take corrective action or begin planning to replace the component in a scheduled manner. As we go down the P-F curve, we can see that it becomes easier and easier to detect the defect. However, we have less and less time to act before the failure, the F point.

Proactive maintenance is about the actions we take in our periodic maintenance activities and adjustments. The intent is to keep the asset in a condition that prevents the failure mode from occurring. Let me say that again: it prevents failure mode. As shown in the example, the belts and pulleys would last longer, and a simple adjustment would prevent these failure modes from progressing. That means we eliminate the failure altogether or at least extend the time to where the failure mode eventually occurs due to the designed end of life.

Other examples include:

- Keeping lubricants clean and applied at the correct quantities and frequencies significantly extend the life of components.
- Correct alignment procedures prevent

the vibrations that can lead to rotating component failures.

- Keeping components clean prevents corrosion, vibration, and overheating caused by working in dirty conditions.
- Performing a weld correctly prevents the need for repeat welds.
- Operating the machine within the correct limits prevents overload-related failures.

In chapter six, we will discuss some of these in more detail and how the mindset of the tradie is the key ingredient to proactive maintenance.

Many who have only worked in a reactive workplace will say proactive maintenance is unrealistic. They will point to the dust, snow, temperature fluctuations, and other harsh conditions that are common in bulk material processing, mining, and other industries, and use them as an excuse to continue accepting the breakdown culture. I understand we cannot have pristine equipment all the time in these challenging environments. But taking care of the equipment during scheduled PM activities to minimise the impact of these environmental factors is essential to improving the equipment reliability and reducing maintenance costs. We once calculated the cost of keeping metal structures clean and painted over decades vs. replacing the steel when it had corroded beyond repair. It turned out significantly more cost-effective to sandblast, paint, and clean these structures than replace them after 30 or 40 years.

Now, you might be thinking, *This is all good if you're doing day-to-day maintenance, but I work on installation* or, *I just do replacements and projects.* Fair enough. But here's the thing – installation and replacement work is just as critical as maintenance work when it comes to reliability. It may be even more so, because you're setting the conditions from the start. In the same way remove and install procedures are critical in maintenance, installation and quality fit-out are crucial for eliminating the onset of failures from the start.

Every time you install a component, you are influencing how long that asset will last. If it is done right – clean, aligned, critical bolts torqued – and with care, that machine or system starts its life strong. But if it is rushed, done roughly, or carelessly, you are planting the seeds of future breakdowns. Someone down the line will be pulling it apart early, wondering why it did not last. And often, the answer goes straight back to the install.

Installation work is also about reliability; it is just happening at the front end. And the end user, whether it is a production operator or a customer in another industry, feels the difference. When things run smoothly, when they last and do not rattle themselves to bits in 6 months, that is the mark of a quality install job.

So if you are doing installs, replacements, or project work, do not think you are out of the reliability game. You are in it up to your neck. Do the job well, and you will be remembered for all the right reasons.

WHY DOES PROACTIVE MAINTENANCE REQUIRE A CULTURE?

I was at an iron ore mine many years ago, and I noticed an electrical switchboard. All of the signs over the push buttons and switches had been cleaned. If you know about an iron ore mine, the orange dust gets into everything and stains all exposed surfaces. On this particular board, all the signs were clearly legible, but there were many other boards on that site where the signs were no longer legible, which could cause problems when people need to operate the equipment controlled by the buttons.

When developing a maintenance program, it would be difficult to determine how often to clean the signs on the board. Boards in different locations would require different frequencies. While this is a very simple example, it does show why it is important for people to be on the lookout for conditions that will cause the component to fail and take action to correct them, and it demonstrates why it needs to be part of the culture, rather than leaving it only to checklists to tell people what needs to be done. It is not just ticking the boxes on a preventative maintenance checklist. The signs on that board will last for the life of the board if kept clean. Other illegible signs that have not been maintained could cause problems for operators and will require replacement.

This same concept can be used for any equipment that operates in harsh environments with variable contamination, temperature, or dynamic loading. No single checklist can account for variable conditions. It requires a culture of people who perform inspections to notice these conditions and take proactive action when required.

AIRLINE MECHANICS

The airline industry employs the concept of a general visual inspection (GVI) task, in which the technician is required to look only for conditions that require restoration. These GVI tasks are in addition to those known to address specific failure modes. They are just visual inspections to identify obvious damage, failure, or irregularity so proactive action can be taken.

Years after my trade experience, when I worked in a central maintenance improvement role, I took a team to study how airline maintenance teams worked. There is a lot at stake in mining and other asset-intensive industries, but the stakes in commercial aviation are even higher. People's lives are on the line, and even little mistakes can have a devastating impact on the public's perception of flying and airlines in general. I thought the maintenance and reliability improvement teams in aviation might have a few things to teach us.

What we learnt was the aviation industry has many of the same systems and processes we have in mining and heavy industry. Planning, scheduling, condition monitoring, reliability teams, they are all there. Nothing is radically different on paper, and some of the documentation of their processes is less advanced than ours.

What *is* different is the mindset. The airline industry has an absolute, non-negotiable commitment to high-quality work execution and proactive maintenance. Every bolt, inspection, and checklist is treated with intricate focus. That is the key difference I found. Yes, their MSG-3 (maintenance steering group-3) discipline also produces very comprehensive equipment strategies, but our industries have also developed similar approaches using RCM (reliability-centred maintenance) theory with little or no sustainable improvement.

They have not beaten us with better reliability processes and theory. Instead, they have beaten us with better follow-through and work execution standards. For example, on this excursion, they told us about a technician who had to replace a hydraulic hose on the landing gear of a large aircraft. The spare hose was not included with the kit, but the technician found one that looked identical. It was identical, except for the pressure rating. He replaced the hose, and when the plane landed, that hose blew out. No one was injured, but it was a significant unscheduled failure. This technician was immediately stood down pending investigation. In the end, he was able to remain employed but was demoted and had to spend 2 more years working his way back up to the same level, because in the airline industry, all jobs must be done exactly right, with no room for ad hoc repair practices like these.

I debated whether to share this story, as I do not want to give the impression that we should penalise tradies who make mistakes and cause breakdowns. I do not advocate that course of action. However, creating the right culture will significantly improve our practices. Reactive cultures result from misguided leadership, but if we could get our trades teams to execute critical maintenance activities to the same standard as the aviation industry, the reliability of our equipment would significantly improve, not because we changed our systems, but because we raised the standard of what is acceptable when critical tasks are done or when action is taken to correct defects. For example, we can require double sign-off of critical alignment or bolting tasks, clear standards of when corrective or restorative action is required on leaks, or establish a clear process to restore to the original design condition so a temporary repair does not become a permanent repair.

KEY TAKEAWAYS

Fixing things when they are small costs much less than waiting until they become big problems or replacing components that wear out prematurely. The economics of proactive work have been proven many times over, yet I still see the majority of the industries I have been involved in not taking action to correct small defects or conditions that could lead to defects developing.

Creating a proactive maintenance culture requires discussing situations at the relevant meetings. If the situation with the belts being left loose was discussed at a meeting, everyone would have learnt that it is not only better for the business to make the small adjustments, but it is also better for the tradies, as they will not have to fix as many breakdowns.

6

TLC and TCDC: Priorities for Mechanical, Electrical, and Welding Tradies

"TIGHT, LUBRICATED, CLEAN. TIGHT, CLEAN, DRY, COOL. THE SMALLEST HABITS CAN PREVENT THE BIGGEST BREAKDOWNS."

A few years ago, I was working on a site where the trucks seemed to be continually breaking down. It was not the engine. It was not the hydraulics. It was not even the control systems. The biggest source of downtime, again and again, was hydraulic stairs. You know, the ones that let you climb safely onto the machine. Every week, they would jam, misalign, or fail to deploy properly and stop the truck.

What was the maintenance strategy? Test the stairs during the service. That was it. Just a function check. But the operator used the stairs multiple times a shift, so a simple function test added no value whatsoever. It did not stop breakdowns; it did not prevent failures, and it certainly did not reduce downtime.

We looked more closely and found no proactive maintenance tasks. No hydraulic fluid checks. No cleaning of the control box. No inspection or adjustment of limit switches. No torque check on fasteners. We added a handful of basic tasks – nothing expensive, nothing new or complex – and within 3 months, the breakdowns stopped. Completely.

That is what mechanical reliability looks like, and it starts with three words: tight, lubricated, and clean, or TLC. Using a TLA (three-letter acronym) helps us remember these simple principles to apply during our maintenance and servicing tasks. In the same way TCDC (tight, clean, dry, and cool) helps us remember the fundamentals of electrical maintenance, TLC is the bedrock of mechanical quality.

MECHANICAL TRADIE PRIORITIES
Tight – Bolted, Clamped, Secured

Ask any experienced fitter, and they will tell you: loose components are the beginning of mechanical death. Loose bolts, loose guards, loose mounts, and loose clamps do not fail on their own. They cause vibration. Vibration causes misalignment. Misalignment causes wear, fatigue, or cracking. And that is when your breakdown happens.

Doing quality work means taking the time to secure every connection to the right torque, or at least the critical connections to the right torque and all other connections tightly. It means checking the fasteners on guards and clamps to ensure nothing is rattling loose.

I was once on a site, and three fitters were replacing bolts on a large coupling between two shafts that were driving a large rotating drum. I asked the fitters why they were replacing the bolts. They said they kept breaking.

When I asked them what torque the new bolts had to be tightened to, they said, "Bloody tight, mate," and continued with the flogging spanner and hammer! No wonder the bolts kept breaking. While this was likely the time to use a torque wrench, other connections are fine to just be done bloody tight. Walking around with a torque wrench rather than a rattle gun, or at least having both tools available, is something to consider.

There are many detailed textbooks on how to do quality bolted connections, and it is something to always keep at the front of your mind.

Lubricated – the Lifeblood of Every Moving Part

If there is one thing that extends component life more than anything, it is proper lubrication. But here is the catch: 'greased' does not mean 'lubricated'. I have seen machines with broken auto-grease lines, grease nipples so caked with dirt that no grease ever gets through, and tanks that are empty but ticked off as 'okay'.

Proactive mechanical maintenance means:

- Grease lines are inspected and replaced when damaged.
- Grease points are cleaned before application.
- Oil levels are checked, *and* the oil condition is verified.
- Filters are replaced at the correct intervals, not "whenever someone remembers".

When we talk about lubrication, we are talking about *preserving life*. Get it right, and your bearings, bushes, pins, seals, and gears will run smoothly for years. Get it wrong, and they will grind themselves into scrap.

Again, there are many programs and textbooks to learn more about quality lubrication. The intent here is to ensure mechanical tradies keep this front of mind also.

Clean – Because Dirt Destroys Machines

Dirt is not just dirt; it is a contaminant. It holds moisture, causes abrasion, hides leaks, and wears seals. In mechanical systems, dirt is a silent destroyer.

One of the most overlooked maintenance tasks is a proper cleanout of key areas, especially hydraulic control boxes, gear housings, inspection ports, build-up around components, cooling systems, and underbody cavities. Every mechanical tradie should be equipped to clean out the areas they maintain. It is not about polishing paint; it is about keeping the machine in a state where defects are visible and conditions are not causing degradation of the equipment.

Clean machines are reliable machines. Dirty machines are hiding their defects.

TLC in Action – Why It Works

The TLC mindset is not about doing more tasks; it is about always doing the small tasks that prevent the onset of the big tasks. The stairs example from earlier shows how simple TLC tasks – such as tightening, checking fluid condition, cleaning, and adjusting limit switches – can eliminate the most common cause of downtime. No project, no budget. Just a quality mindset applied properly.

The TLC mindset creates reliability and saves time and money in the short, medium, and long term.

Why TLC Needs to Be Routine

Doing this once will not help. Like brushing your teeth, you have got to do it regularly. Maintenance routines must be structured around TLC. Every time you work on a component, ask yourself:

- Is it tight?
- Is it lubricated?
- Is it clean?

If the answer to any of these is, "I don't know," then it is not a quality job. Yet. We cannot keep pretending reactive fixes will get us ahead. The only way to stay ahead of breakdowns is to never let the failure mode begin. That is what proactive mechanical maintenance really is.

ELECTRICAL TRADIE PRIORITIES
TC ✗ DC Is the Key

When it comes to electrical reliability, there is one principle that will eliminate more failures than any technology, system, or strategy: *keep it tight, clean, dry, and cool.* I call it **TCDC,** and yeah, it sounds a bit like AC-DC. That is deliberate. It makes it easier to remember, and let's face it, it sparks a bit more interest than 'electrical maintenance fundamentals'.

Many years ago, I was leading electrical maintenance at a materials handling and processing plant. There were often hot joints within the electrical drive motor junction boxes. I wondered why this was occurring, and I realised that, as part of the site maintenance program, there was a practice of opening these junction boxes every 6 months, removing all of the cables from the terminals, and testing the motor winding continuity and insulation. This practice was causing the hot electrical connections. We stopped this, drew a diagram showing how the motor terminals should be connected (that is, with the cables connected so current does not pass through the bolted connection itself), and then issued all the electrical tradies a very small torque wrench, since the terminals were mainly 5 mm brass bolts. These wrenches were so cute. Tightening the bolts in the correct sequence and then using a small torque wrench to ensure the best possible connection eliminated all of the failures we were experiencing. We also developed a method to test the winding insulation from the control room without undoing any connections so we could be forewarned of any insulation degradation.

So what does TCDC actually mean?

Tight – Because Loose Means Trouble

Loose terminals, lugs, and connections are one of the most common causes of electrical breakdowns, and they are entirely preventable. Heat build-up, arcing, nuisance trips, sensor faults – it all starts with something not being tight. With electrical connections, the tension applied to connections is all the more sensitive. Years ago, we suffered a lot of bad connections and intermittent trips because people were over-tensioning the screws in terminals. Copper conductor is soft and easy to over-tension. When this occurs, the strands of wire break and create a loose connection that heats up and causes these problems.

If you are not doing electrical connections with precision and care, then you are not working in a proactive manner.

We do not need to over-engineer this. Every tradie should carry a torque wrench and be confident using it to manufacturer specs, as well as follow the correct procedures for connecting crimp lugs or any of the multitude of other electrical connections. Hand-tight or close enough is not good enough when you are trying to build reliable electrical connections, especially in plants with some level of vibration.

Clean – Because Dirt Is a Conductor in Disguise

Dust, oil, grime, none of it belongs in electrical gear. I have lost count of how many breakdowns were traced back to gunked-up limit switches, dirty relays, or enclosures that had not been cleaned in years. Dirt compromises insulation, causes corrosion, and can even bridge terminals in extreme cases.

One of the most neglected pieces of proactive maintenance is simply cleaning the gear properly. Panels, terminations, motor junction boxes – wipe them, blow them out with clean air or vacuum where required, and take pride in how they look. If it looks neglected, it usually is.

Dry– Because Moisture Invites Failure

Moisture is the enemy of everything electrical. It causes

corrosion, promotes short circuits, and wrecks insulation resistance. The thing is, moisture issues are rarely a surprise. They stem from obvious conditions: missing gaskets, damaged glands, poor cabinet seals, and open holes from mod jobs that were not finished properly.

Remember the old trick of removing a button and just leaving a hole in the panel? I have seen that too many times. The rain gets in; the dust follows, and suddenly you have got a tripping circuit or failed controller.

You are not just maintaining circuits – you are protecting them from the environment. That means resealing, reglanding, and replacing what has perished. If it is wet, it will eventually fail, guaranteed.

Cool – Because Overheating Kills Components Quietly

Heat kills electronics slowly and silently – until they just stop. And often, by the time they fail, they have taken a few other components with them. Transformers, drives, PLCs – they all need proper cooling, ventilation, and spacing to dissipate heat. Fans clogged with dust, vents blocked by rags or stored tools are the silent killers we walk past every day.

One of the best things you can do during PMs is check airflow. Are the fans spinning freely? Are the filters clean? Is there anything restricting natural convection? You do not need a degree in thermodynamics to prevent heat failures. You just need eyes open and a mindset that says, "If it's hot, find out why."

Some years ago, I was investigating inverter failures. They were failing at around half their design life. It was impossible to determine the exact cause, but it was put down to excessive heat. The insulation inside the inverter modules themselves was failing. During this investigation, I learnt that the life of electrical insulation decreases exponentially as temperature increases. There is a rule called Montsinger's Rule, which states that for every 10°C rise in operating temperature, insulation life roughly halves. It does not take too much build-up of dust or contaminants to cause a 10°C rise in operating temperature.

The Vehicle Horn Example

Let me give you an example of what not to do when you are aiming for proactive electrical maintenance. It is a practice I have seen across multiple sites, and it is frustrating because it is practically useless: testing the horn on mobile equipment during a service.

Think about it. The operator tests the horn ten times a day. What are we achieving by pressing it once during a service? We are not preventing anything.

What we *should* do is apply TCDC:

- **Tight:** Are the horn wires and mounting bolts without any looseness?
- **Clean:** Are the horn housing and wiring free from mud, grease, or debris?
- **Dry:** Are the cable entries sealed from moisture ingress?
- **Cool:** Has something changed that could increase its temperature, such as a ventilation path being blocked or a build-up of debris around the unit?

It does not matter if you still want to test the horn, but testing it without doing these other tasks is useless. The TCDC tasks are proactive maintenance that prevent failure.

Why TCDC Matters More Than Ever

In modern systems, electrical failures often mean whole-machine failures. Sensors, PLCs, and communication lines – all of it stops when the electrical systems fail. And we have all seen how long it can take to diagnose those issues if the failure was not apparent. That is downtime nobody can afford.

TCDC is about *condition management,* not *condition monitoring.* It is not a new technology or system – it is old-school care done to a high standard, consistently.

The beauty of this approach is that it does not require extra budget, special tools, or a new strategy. It just requires commitment to the basics, executed with pride, precision, and repeatability.

WELDING TRADIE PRIORITIES

One area that has always caused me to ask questions is welding cracks in plant and equipment, especially in mobile equipment under dynamic forces. Cracks are not usually a significant cause of unscheduled downtime, as they are relatively easy to monitor and repair. However, if left too long or in a difficult location, they can cause large unscheduled downtime events.

Often, when I look at equipment, I see areas of the structures (handrails, access ways, and even structural body or booms) where the cracks continue to get repaired time and again. See the example below, which is not uncommon in some areas. Yet, when repaired correctly, the area should not recrack, or it should at least take a very long time before the crack reappears due to overloading.

The fact is, however, when you look at the equipment, you can easily see areas that have been continually repaired. If the repairs were done correctly the first time, you would not recognise it. The welds would be ground smooth, blended into the base material, and stress-relieved.

I learnt a bit about welding correctly when I was in charge of a mining fleet and we had a LeTourneau loader. The right-hand lifting arm broke in half, and there were no spare arms, as they are not meant to break in service like that. If you saw these arms, you would wonder how it could happen. When we investigated, we found that there was no adequate inspection regime in that area, but we still had to fix the problem. We used the OEM to complete the repairs the first time, but it cracked again and was back in the shop about 2 months later. However, this time we picked up the crack before it totally broke the arm in half, as we had implemented an inspection regime.

The second time, though, I was introduced to a welding expert who said it should not recrack like that if the repair were done correctly. I engaged their organisation to design an effective repair process and weld procedures, and supervise the quality of the work. This repair lasted 18 months before it started to crack, and the cracks were very small initially, allowing us to respond in a controlled manner. At this time, we learnt that the cracks were due to frequent overloading of the machine while it was working on the loading face. By conducting high-quality welds and controlling operating practices, we mitigated the problem's severity. Eventually, we eliminated the issue entirely by controlling overloading.

I learnt so much about quality welding through this experience. It is an area where there are huge opportunities for improvement and for eliminating rework. I thought it best, however, to engage with experts in this area, so I asked the guys from Welding Quality Management Systems (WQMS) to write a section on the topic. Simon and the team at WQMS have done some very practical work to make real improvements in maintenance welding knowledge and practices.

I have also found the welding trades to be the most related to a craft, even to this day. Simply having a qualification in welding does not mean a tradie can do an effective job at all welding tasks. It requires specialist knowledge and years of experience. Thank you, Simon, for writing the following section on maintenance welding.

MAINTENANCE WELDING
Types of Maintenance Welding

There are five general types of maintenance welding, depending on the damage mechanism, severity, and the type of component or equipment.

Each has its own distinct objectives and methodologies:

- **Crack repairs:** This is the most common form of maintenance welding. It involves restoring the structural integrity of components that have developed fatigue cracks. Fatigue cracking occurs in many types of equipment in the mining, marine, industrial, civil, transport, and defence sectors that are subjected to cyclic stresses.

- **Hardfacing:** The application of a wear-resistant material to a surface by welding. This technique is used to extend the service life of components subject to abrasion, impact, or erosion wear mechanisms.

- **Upgrades and modifications:** Sometimes engineering modifications to the original design are required to address problems or to provide increased service capacity to meet operational requirements. Modifications must only be made with proper engineering analysis and approval. Whoever authorises modifications assumes the design responsibilities under the law.

- **Replacement:** In cases where a section of a structure or component is severely damaged, it is sometimes feasible to replace that section. This involves cutting out the damaged section and welding in a new one.

- **Compliance:** Some equipment is regulated by standards and codes of practice. This is basically everything that is safety-related, used for lifting, or contains pressure. Repair of these types of equipment must comply with the design standard specifications.

Fatigue cracking is particularly problematic, as its effects can range from nuisance to catastrophic failures. Severe cracks require emergency repairs to prevent failure. Chronic fatigue cracking reduces viable structural life, requiring major rebuilding or refurbishments, shutdowns, or premature component replacement. Fatigue cracking can occur in many types of compliance-based plant and equipment, such as cranes, ROPS/FOPS (roll-over protective structures/falling-object protective structures), lifting jigs, mine winders, and pressure piping.

Maintenance Welding Objectives and Risk Management

The fundamental objective of maintenance welding is to achieve an effective repair. An effective repair restores functionality and integrity, does not modify the original design, does not introduce any new risks or failure modes, and most importantly, lasts. For fatigue crack repairs, an effective repair should last at least as long as it took to crack from new, or even longer.

Maintenance welding is substantially different from the fabrication of new structures and equipment. Specific knowledge and skills are required to identify the defect, prepare and perform the repair, achieve the repair objective, and manage the technical risks associated with the repair. Poorly done crack repairs can have big consequences. In the worst case, it may be a catastrophic failure that kills someone. Other times, it will typically result in rapid recracking, requiring more repairs and more downtime. The simple truth is there are very different risks to manage when fixing things than when making them.

It is generally not appropriate to use fabrication-based standards, such as AS/NZS 1554, for structural maintenance welding – they simply do not provide a suitable framework to manage the specific risks and achieve the repair objective. Maintenance welding also has different safety hazards than fabrication. It is also essential to know there are not any standards for maintenance welding – the 'repairs' in structural welding standards only apply to the rectification of welding defects from fabrication!

In this chapter, you will learn the ingredients for achieving effective fatigue crack repairs. This is not about following specific welding procedures or anything like that. And it is not as simple as, "V out the defect and weld it up!" Effective repairs require applying fundamental principles, understanding what is important and why, competent welders, and simple frameworks for repair methodologies.

Management of Maintenance Welding

A systematic approach is essential for managing maintenance welding to achieve effective repairs. The diagram on the next page shows the steps and factors to consider in the repair management process. Start at the outside ring, working towards the centre.

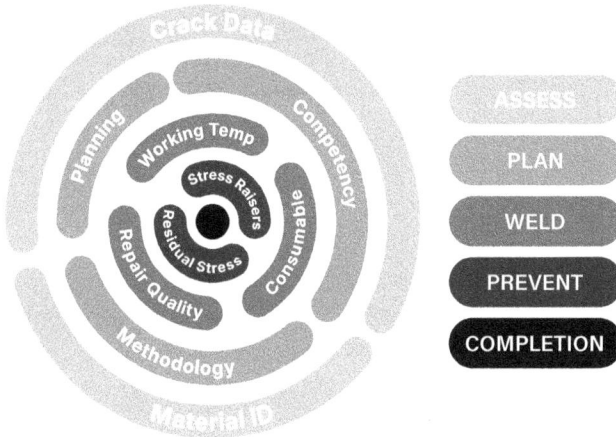

Assess = Assess Repair Requirements

Before any welding commences, a thorough assessment is crucial to understand the nature and extent of the crack and the material properties.

- **Crack data:**
  - » Location and orientation of the crack.
  - » Length and depth of the crack.
  - » Evidence of crack growth or arrest.
  - » Presence of multiple cracks.
  - » Use the *crack data system* nomenclature.

- **Material type:**
  - » Identification of the base material (for example, carbon steel, stainless steel, aluminum alloy).
  - » Understand its metallurgical properties, weldability, and susceptibility to cracking.
  - » Previous repair history and material degradation.

Plan = Develop a Repair Plan

A comprehensive repair plan ensures all necessary resources are available and the repair is executed safely and effectively.

- **Planning:** Use the TAPE acronym
  - » **Time:** Estimate the time required for set-up, preparation, welding, and post-weld treatment, accounting for potential delays.
  - » **Access:** Determine how to safely and effectively access the repair area, accounting for any confined spaces, or height or environmental challenges.
  - » **Personnel:** Assign qualified and experienced

welders and the necessary support staff (for example, fitters, firewatchers, trades assistants, and so on).

> » **Equipment:** Identify and secure all necessary welding equipment, consumables, preheat/post-weld heat-treatment equipment, and safety gear.

- **Maintenance welder competency:** Ensure the assigned welders possess the necessary knowledge and skills for the repair at hand. The required competency level is based on the repair difficulty.

- **Repair methodology:** Each repair requires an appropriate methodology based on the crack's characteristics, material type, and operational requirements. This includes decisions on joint preparation type and shape, welding process used, specific methodology based on the type of cracking, residual stress control, and fatigue-life improvement methods. Be prepared to adapt or modify the plan on site if unexpected conditions arise during the repair, while still maintaining safety and quality standards.

Weld = Perform Repair Welding

This stage involves the actual execution of the welding repair, adhering to the established plan and quality control measures.

- **Set-up:** Proper preparation of the workpiece and welding equipment is essential. This includes cleaning, ensuring a stable welding environment, and safety considerations.
- **Working temperature:** Maintain the temperature within the preheat and interpass ranges to prevent hard heat-affected zones (HAZ).
- **Consumable:** Select the correct welding consumable for the base material, considering strength, ductility, and hydrogen content.
- **Prevent hydrogen cracking:**
  - » Remove sources of hydrogen.
  - » Minimise residual stresses.
  - » Use the correct working temperature to prevent hard HAZ formation.
  - » When in doubt, bake it out (heat up to 200°C for a couple of hours).

Prevent = Prevent Recracking

Preventative measures must be taken to minimise the likelihood of future cracking at or near the repair site.

- **Residual stress control:**
  » **Minimise repair volume:** Reduce the amount of weld metal deposited to minimise shrinkage stresses.
  » **Weld runs:** Use fewer, larger runs. Work from outside in rather than from one side to the other.
  » **Inter-run peening:** Where feasible, peen each weld pass to relieve residual stresses.
  » **Surface peening:** Apply surface peening to the completed weld to induce beneficial compressive stresses.
- **Remove stress raisers:** Eliminate any sharp corners, notches, or other geometric discontinuities that could act as stress concentrators and initiate new cracks.

Completion = Last Steps After Finishing Repair, Ready for Work Order Close-Out

The final stage involves documentation, inspection, and follow-up to ensure the long-term success of the repair before the work order is closed.

- **Quality control:** Use a suitable basic quality control system for the repairs to record what was done, how, and by whom.
- **Completed repairs or reschedule:** Confirm that all planned repairs have been completed or reschedule any unfinished work.
- **Nondestructive testing (NDT):**
  - » **Ultrasonic testing (UT):** Perform UT at the next scheduled inspection if it cannot be performed immediately after repair.
  - » **Changes to inspection scope:** If backing material was used, the inspection scope may need to be adjusted to include routine UT inspections to check for cracking from the root side.
- **Corrosion protection:** Apply appropriate corrosion protection to the repaired area to prevent environmental degradation.

- **Follow-up:** Schedule follow-up inspections or monitoring, especially for repairs involving backing material or temporary fixes, to ensure long-term integrity.

Maintenance Welder Competency

The quality of all maintenance welding depends on the welder's skill. Systems, procedures, supervision, and inspection will not make the welder better or get you the desired outcome. Maintenance welding is usually grossly underestimated in terms of the knowledge and skill required to achieve effective repairs. Maintenance welding is not taught in a trade certificate. Let this fact sink in. You cannot rely on a tradesperson having a trade certificate, or even fabrication-based welder qualifications, as any indication of a their ability to do crack repairs. Carbon arc gouging, used for crack removal, is generally not taught as part of the trade certificate! Gouging requires a high level of skill to do well, controlling the shape and depth of the preparation and creating a smooth, clean gouge. Poor gouging technique can quickly change the nature of the repair (for example, by blowing through the full plate thickness) and add significant time to grinding the preparation. Also, crack repairs are typically performed using flux core, whereas fabrication uses solid wire. These are quite different processes in terms of the skill and experience required.

That is why Maintenance Welder Competency exists (weldercompetency.com). It is an industry credential that combines training on what to do with demonstrated ability based on actual crack repair scenarios. You can have confidence in a welder with an MWC certificate to properly repair cracking in your critical equipment.

7

Only You Improve Reliability

"WHEN LEADERS VALUE QUALITY AND TRADIES MAKE IT THE CULTURE, ROUTINE RELIABILITY BECOMES THE NORM."

FOR LEADERS

If you take one message from this book, let it be this: **only tradies improve reliability.** Every hour of analysis, every planning meeting, every dashboard, and every strategy improvement mean nothing if the quality of work at the trade level is not consistently to agreed standards. Your job as a leader is to build the environment and culture where quality can thrive.

You cannot put quality in at the end or control it with even more checklists. You can only grow it from the hands and minds that do the work.

When I look back at the best-performing sites I have ever been part of, they all had one thing in common: **a culture in which they knew the equipment condition in detail.** The tradies provided this level of detailed knowledge. Leaders and tradies were having open conversations about standards, workmanship, and what would be done to address known issues.

The steps to build that type of culture are simple but, at the same time, not always easy to implement:

- **Make quality visible:** Use photos, failed parts bins, and open discussions to define the standards.
- **Close the loop on feedback:** If a tradie raises a

defect, act on it or explain why you will not.

- **Own the culture**: The leader sets the tone, but the team must carry it.
- **Reward pride, not heroics**: Celebrate the people who prevent breakdowns, not the ones who fix them fast.

Follow these steps, and you will not just improve your KPIs, but you will also build a workplace where people want to stay and perform. That is the real mark of leadership, and it will help you grow your career and influence.

The next step is to put this thinking in the hands of every tradie. Let them see that quality is not a management slogan but a personal standard and part of the culture. Use this thinking in your shift meetings, inductions, and training. Make it the language of your site, and make this book part of your tradies' toolkit!

If you want reliability improvement that lasts, this is how you get it. It starts with the culture. And the culture starts with you.

FOR TRADIES

If you are a tradie, know this: **you are the difference.** Reliability does not live in the office; it lives in your hands and your mind. You are the one who sees the condition, feels the fit, hears the noise, and decides whether the job is done right or done rough. You are the last line before reliability – and the first person who can make it better.

The best tradies I have ever worked with all had the same habits. They:

- Took pride in doing the job properly, not just getting it done.
- Saw problems early and fixed them before they became breakdowns.
- Gave clear feedback, so the next person had better information, and communicated openly with leadership.
- Never walked past something that was not right.

The tradies' mindset is knowing:

- **Tight, lubricated, clean** (for mechanics) and **tight, clean, dry, cool** (for sparkies) will stop most failures before they start.

- **Fix it forever, do not be forever fixing.**
- **If you see it, raise it.** Defects do not fix themselves.
- **Temporary repairs need a follow-up.**
- **Quality work is cheaper, safer, and more satisfying.**

This is the foundation of being a craftsperson and not just a worker. It is what earns respect from your mates, your leaders, and most importantly, yourself.

WHAT ABOUT ROBOTS?

Some may believe that tradespeople will be replaced by robots in the near future. While automation and technology are advancing rapidly, the reality is that tradies will remain irreplaceable for a long time yet. Robots excel at repetitive, highly controlled tasks, but they struggle with the unpredictable nature of maintenance work. Diagnosing faults, adapting to real-world conditions, and applying sound judgement are critical elements of a tradie's role, and technology cannot yet replicate them.

Even as automation takes on some routine tasks, tradies will increasingly become the skilled operators, troubleshooters, and quality controllers of these systems. The role is evolving, not disappearing. In fact, with the added complexity of automated equipment, the need for skilled tradies who understand both traditional mechanical principles and new digital systems is greater than ever. Someone will always have to fix the robots!

MY FINAL WORDS TO YOU

Wherever you go, carry the ideas in this book with you. Use them to lift your standards and your pride in the trade. Talk about quality at every opportunity. Make it visible, because when you do, you make your site better, your team stronger, and your job more rewarding.

Only tradies improve reliability. You are proof of it every day.

FURTHER READING

For some, reading this book may ignite a desire to read more. When I started reading more business and self-improvement books in my late teens, it ignited a passion to read as many as I could. I came across a book with a list of other books the author recommended, so I read them all.

For those who want to read more about working in great cultures and achieving greater career satisfaction, I recommend these books.

- *The Knowing Doing Gap: How Smart Companies Turn Knowledge into Action,* by Jeffrey Pfeffer and Robert I Sutton, Harvard Business Review Press.
- *The 7 Habits of Highly Effective People,* by Stephen R Covey, Simon & Schuster.
- *Who Moved My Cheese?: An Amazing Way to Deal with Change in Your Work and in Your Life,* by Spencer Johnson, Vermilion.
- *Simplicity,* by Edward de Bono, Penguin.
- *Serious Creativity: Using the Power of Lateral Thinking to Create New Ideas,* by Edward de Bono, HarperCollins.

ACKNOWLEDGEMENTS

The tradies who challenged and supported me through my early years as an electrical supervisor, and whose focus on quality work underpinned every reliability gain, long before anyone used the term 'reliability improvement'.

The photos in this book are inspired by Irving Penn, who created the Small Trades series of photos in 1950 and 1951 in Paris, London, and New York. He created these photos as a tribute to skilled workers at a time when many traditional trades were disappearing, and he sought to document and elevate these overlooked individuals. In a similar way, I want to elevate the recognition of the trades' roles in our industries today, as they are critical and will remain so for many years to come.

Also, I must acknowledge and thank Thiess, which is the world's largest mining services provider. Thiess has long been dedicated to quality maintenance, and they do a lot to promote and grow trade skills and apprenticeships across the industry. Thiess also allowed us to take photos of some of their tradespeople at one of their component rebuild workshops. Some of these photos are included in this book.

ABOUT THE AUTHOR

During his engineering career, Gerard Wood became passionate about two things: practical asset management and quality work by tradies. After 40 years in maintenance, from starting as a tradie to leading asset management across entire businesses and assisting multiple companies sustainably improve their reliability, he has seen what really drives reliability, and it is not reports, dashboards, or meetings. It is skilled people doing the right work, the right way. That is the engine room of reliability performance.

Through decades of helping sites lift their game, Gerard came to a simple realisation: nothing improves reliability faster than quality trades work backed by practical, no-nonsense maintenance leadership. That is the heartbeat of his coaching and his books, *Simplifying Mining Maintenance* and *Only Tradies Improve Reliability.* He keeps it sharp, straight-talking, and yeah, he likes to share a few laughs too.

Gerard would love this book to positively impact 1 million tradies, helping them gain more job satisfaction, feel proud to be part of a successful team, and get their businesses to perform better.

When he started in the consulting game, he also wanted to make a positive difference in the industries he worked in, but he soon realised he needed to reach a larger and broader audience to make a more significant difference. Hence, he turned his attention to using media, books, and online platforms to share his experience and help more people improve faster and benefit from the experiences he was fortunate to have during his career.

gerardwood.com.au

TURBO LEADERSHIP COACHING

1:1 LEADERSHIP COACHING

 A full-year engagement with Gerard, starting with some prep work and a one-week onsite intensive, supported by structured tools, monthly check-ins, and weekly content via our coaching app.

TURBO LEADERSHIP IN YOUR POCKET

 Prefer to go solo? Subscribe to the app for structured leadership training designed specifically for those in maintenance and asset management roles.

Perfect for frontline leaders or trade-based teams. Available individually or in bulk for company-wide development.

Play store   Apple store

GALLERY

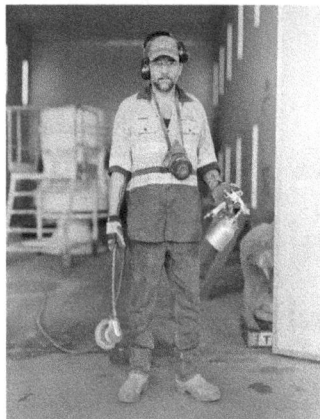

GALLERY

AUDIOBOOK

Great news! *Only Tradies Improve Reliability* is also available in audio format. Jump onto your favourite audiobook platform now and check it out.